PURE GIFT

THE SECOND COMING OF JESUS

Pura Regalado

CHAPTER 1

Humanity is ignoring Dr, Carl Gustav Jung's theory of the collective unconscious. This theory is not even mentioned in investigations of the unknown which are in fact the manifestations of an archetype that emanated from our collective unconscious created by collective beliefs, myths or legends. I am a firsthand witness to the manifestation of what Dr. Jung called the negative dynamic archetype that tried to possess me to turn me into a senseless mass killer. With my high moral integrity and sound mind I overcame my ordeal with this satanic force. Had Satan triumphed in possessing me, I would have been the first in the list of school senseless mass killers because my bout with Satan happened on the last three months of 1975, when I was a college professor teaching Architectural subjects in my alma mater Mapua Institute of Technology in Manila Philippines. My ordeal was like being swallowed alive by an evil dragon and tortured in its belly for three long horrendous months but the vile in the belly of this evil dragon failed to digest me and it was forced to vomit me out back to my normal self to bear witness to the fact that there is truly Satan who possesses the morally bankrupt and the mentally impaired to become senseless mass killers and there is truly God who came to save me when Satan found my weakness and I was forced to surrender. God clarified to me in visions Dr. Jung's theory of the collective unconscious confirming its profoundness.

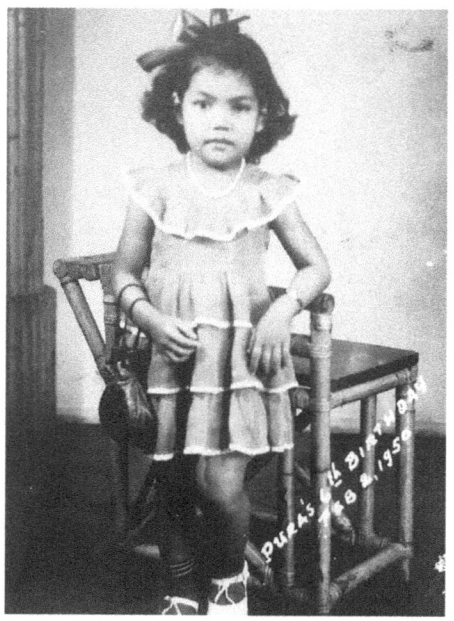

Pura @ 6

I understand that it is not easy to believe something you did not experience but please consider all the facts of my life before you give your judgement. Jesus appeared to me and made me aware that I was born with all the signs of his second coming, I was born the second child, the second daughter, on the second hour of the second day of the second month while the second World War was raging. My mother was born when all of Christendom was celebrating the birth of Jesus, on Christmas day, December 25, 1922, and my year of birth was 22 years later, 1944. Many more pattern of 2 incidents came upon my life repeatedly. The moment I was made aware of the significance of the pattern of 2, its occurrence came more in rapid succession reminding me that I have a task to fulfill and I believe the pattern of 2 will keep appearing to me until I fulfill my task, the task of imparting to humanity the true purpose of life. Even all my sister's names are related to Jesus; My older sister is Milagros - miracles, my younger sister is Anita, diminutive of Ann, the name of the mother of Mary, grandmother of Jesus and my youngest sister is Elizabeth - the name of the cousin of Mary. I was baptized Pura Regalado y Cailao. Pura Regalado in English is Pure Gift. Cailao, my mother's last name phonetically in Tagalog is Kailaw – one who also brought light. I am, therefore, Pure Gift, one who also brought light. Regalado is my father's family name, which in Spanish is the past tense for regalo or gift in English. I was born on February 2, which in the Catholic calendar is the feast day of the purification of the blessed virgin Mary, so purification was shortened to Pura, my first name.

In the event of September 11, 2001, numerologists observed several numerological instances that equated to the number 11: the actual day number is 11, the first plane to hit the towers was Flight 11, it had 92 people on board - 9+2=11, and so forth. All these repeated patterns of number 11 are listed on Numerology of September 11 on the internet. No one saw the true significance of this pattern of the number 11 repeated over and over but when Richard, my officemate emailed this information to me for the first time, I had goose bumps all over because I immediately saw the fact that number eleven is two number ones and 1+1=2, a pattern that is repeatedly occurring in my life. Another hair raiser to me was the fact that the year 2001 is the year 1422 in the calendar of the terrorists that perpetrated the 9/11 incident, a fact that clearly bears the pattern of 2. There were two massive towers that collapsed; there were two sites of destructions, the World Trade Center and the Pentagon. The American President at that time was George Bush the second and the monarch of its most important ally was Queen Elizabeth the second. That was the time Jesus appeared to me.

In his Gospels, Jesus said that a witness will come for him, I am that witness, I witnessed his second coming and I wrote the messages of his second coming on my Facebook pages – The Power of the mind where I laid out proof of the profoundness of Dr. Carl Gustav Jung's theory of the collective unconscious, followed by my other FB page – The Second Coming of Jesus. I disseminated the messages of the second coming of Jesus available for all for free and I even boosted its dissemination at my own expense until Facebook forbade me from boosting them because to criticize any religion is against their policy. I self-published this book after getting disappointed that these messages are not disseminated to humanity fast enough through Facebook. The only reason I added other details of my life is to make this manuscript long enough to be a book.

Jesus said that the only sign that shall be given to an evil and adulterous generation is the sign of Jonah. Our generation is indeed evil and adulterous. Jesus told me that the ordeal I went through with the allegorical evil dragon that swallowed me, which I overcame, back to my freedom to bear witness to the fact that there is indeed a Supreme Power above who saved me and He is waiting for us to reach perfection to join Him in eternal life; and there is indeed Satan who is anti-life who wants us all to be evil so that we will become the dirt of the earth, dead forever, to maintain this physical universe.

Jesus said: The Queen from the south shall rise for she shall come from the uttermost part of the earth and shall condemn them. The Philippines where I was born is an uttermost place from where Jesus walked on earth and God sent me to condemn all false beliefs, false prophets and false gods. In a dream, I was told that I was Catherine of Aragon in my past incarnation, which felt so real, I was wearing a tight queenly voluminous garb which was hampering my movements. I died of a broken heart in that incarnation but in this present one, I survived the anguish of having a philandering husband. It was during this dream as Queen Catherine of Aragon that a big antique key was dropped before me. It was a puzzle for me at that time but now I know it is the key to open the door where we can cast Satan to perdition. Satan is none other than the negative dynamic archetype that emanates from our collective unconscious created by all evil, perverse, malicious, selfish, corrupt, false and superstitious beliefs and all negative destructive thought energies of man. If you nurture any of these evil thoughts your thought energies are adding to the force of Satan.

Jesus said that you will come by one bearing a pitcher of water, enter the house he enters in. I am an Aquarian, the water bearer, Jesus bade you to believe me. Jesus said in his letter to a Muslim church in Pergamos: You hold the doctrine of Balaam. God showed me while I was at the foot of the Mayan temple Uxmal, that the god of Balaam required human sacrifice just like the god of the Mayans who is also the false god who told Abraham to kill his son as sacrifice. In this same letter of Jesus to the church in Pergamos, he also wrote: To one who overcomes shall be given a white stone with a new name. I overcame my sign of Jonah ordeal and God gave me that white stone with letters SPA naturally inscribed in it, SPA is for Supreme Power Above. There are false gods who are Satan in disguise and pagan gods, but the true God is the only Supreme Power Above.

The Secret Bible Code came to light just before the end of the second millennia with the aid of computers, meaning its significance is for our generation. No one saw its true significance, but I know it is God's way of giving credence to the task that is laid on my shoulders. This Secret Bible Code says that the matrix where the word messiah is, also shows the name of Jesus and Pure Gift. I am Pure Gift, one who also brought light. A messiah is a savior, God sent me to save the souls of the deceived followers of the false prophet whose words are leading them to break God's law: DO NOT KILL, which will get their souls cast unto the lake of fire. These followers of the false prophet are so proud to break God's law, they post on the internet gruesome videos of their horrendous act of brutally cutting the neck of the innocents to their death. Anyone proclaiming the false prophet who is the prophet of the false god who told Abraham to kill his son as sacrifice, are emboldening those who are carrying out his violent words to kill infidels to their beliefs, therefore, they too are guilty of the killing. This false prophet claims that he superseded Jesus, and that God will not send another prophet after him because he was the seal of prophets. I am living proof of the blasphemy of this false prophet.

All Abrahamic religions are therefore guilty of the deaths of innocent victims of Islamic terrorism because by professing that the god who told Abraham to kill his son as sacrifice is the true God who is testing the faith of Abraham, the false god that the terrorists are worshipping, they all embolden the terrorist who follow the command of the prophet of this false god to kill infidels to their false beliefs. God is everywhere, we are moving in His realm, He knows what is in our hearts and minds, He does not need to test us. God clearly told me that any god who tell people to kill is Satan in disguise. God clearly told me that He will never contradict His own law – DO NOT KILL. The truth is that the false god who told Abraham to kill his son as sacrifice tried to turn the religion of Abraham into a human sacrifice religion. He failed with Judaism and Christianity but with the help of his prophet, the false prophet, they successfully turned Islam into a human sacrifice religion with the promise of pleasure of the flesh as reward for those who are deceived to be human sacrifice to follow the command: smite the neck of infidels. They are suicide bombers, Muhammad Atta and his crew who attacked New York in September 11, 2001 and many others.

When Nostradamus said that on the seventh month of 1999, a terrible leader from the east shall come from the sky, I wondered if he was referring to me. July of 1999 was the very first time I set foot in Europe. I landed in Rome from the sky on an airplane. I am from the east, the Philippines. If he was referring to me, why did he see me as terrible? Is it because the message I bring unveils all the false beliefs of all organized religions? Is it because I am trying to stop his end of our world prophecy from happening? Was there anything worthy of attention that happened at that time if he was not talking about me?

The message of the Second Coming of Jesus is this: science is the absolute truth and God wants us to live our lives through the scope of science. If science cannot include God yet in its pursuit of knowledge, they must explain all these synchronicities of my life. Through the parable of Jesus of the Sower and the seed, I was shown vivid images of how we, homo sapiens, evolved from a simple celled organism to the intelligent beings that we are now, as these words floated out of the page of the Bible – "Others fell unto good ground, and brought forth fruit, some a hundredfold, some sixtyfold, some thirtyfold. Who hath ears to hear, let him hear." Science has no answer to all questions about our universe, but in my understanding, the visions that God showed me gave answers to some of these questions. In his Gospels, Jesus always said; he that hath an ear let him hear, every time his message is for our generation. Believe it or not, the pages of the Bible opened by itself unto specific pages and the texts that God wanted me to read floated out and were magnified a hundred-fold and I saw vivid images of what they truly mean.

What is the significance of the tale of the fall of Lucifer and his minions where they were cast out of heaven? I have a nagging vision that this was the start of what science calls the Big Bang that started this physical universe where we are, 13.8 billion years ago. I already mentioned that God sowed the seed of life in this physical universe. I was shown that the ultimate purpose of life is to turn physical matter into pure energy to get back to heaven. Why are all ancient religions mostly human sacrifice religions? Is it because Lucifer wants to maintain this physical universe that he is doing everything in his power to prevent life from achieving its ultimate purpose of turning physical matter into energy? He started all the human sacrifice religion such as the false god who tried to turn the religion of Abraham into a human sacrifice religion, commanding him to kill his son as as sacrifice, to keep man earthbound. Lucifer wants us all to be evil and evil thoughts create Satan who possesses the morally bankrupt and mentally impaired to turn them into senseless mass killers so that their souls or consciousness will be terminated to become particles in the magma molecules that oozes out as lava – thus written as – sinner souls cast to the lake of fire in the Bible.

I saw that the body of Jesus turned into pure energy to become one with God body and soul and Jesus said, "Come and follow me."

This is the ultimate purpose of life, to reach the perfection of Jesus and metamorphose body and soul to be one with God in everlasting life. I was shown how all the atoms in the body of Jesus converted into pure energy to become one with God, which in Buddhist terminology is Nirvana. This process of conversion from matter to pure energy generated the heat that burned the image of Jesus in his burial shroud which is on display in a church in Torino, Italy. The image is in the negative because the fabric closest his skin burned the most producing the darkest tint. This shroud had undergone intense scrutiny and experts concluded that no coloring pigment was used to produce the image, they concluded that the image was burned into the fabric, which agrees with the visions I saw. This shroud had been contaminated by human touch for more than a millennia before carbon dating was made, aside from surviving a fire where extreme heat must have affected its molecular structure, therefore it is no longer possible to obtain accurate carbon dating for its age. Anyway, there are paintings depicting the shroud done years before that of the date derived from carbon dating, which proves the inaccuracy of the carbon dating.

The Science Channel repeatedly tried to prove that the shroud of Jesus on display in Torino Italy is fake, the latest I saw was about a blood flow at the back waist of Jesus which they concluded was impossible to happen. They used a mannequin with a supposedly chest wound, mimicking the chest wound of Jesus where he was pierced by a spear where a sizable amount of blood flowed out to the surface where the mannequin was lying down on. There was no blood flow to the back waist of the mannequin because it was unmoving dead flat on its back. The blood flow on the shroud of Jesus is physical proof that Jesus was alive! He turned on his side thus the blood from his chest wound flowed across the back of his waist! Jesus was alive when he reached Nirvana! One needs to be alive to reach Nirvana! The Christian belief that Jesus resurrected from being dead is a blasphemy! Every year,

Christians celebrate the resurrection of Jesus, and they call it Easter. Easter is English for Eostre, the pagan goddess of fertility, eggs are the symbol of birth and bunny rabbits are symbol of prolific procreators. Pagans were celebrating Easter and when they accepted Christianity, they did not give up Eostre, the eggs and the bunnies, they merely merged the 'resurrection' of Jesus with it.

Science cannot explain why our universe is continuously expanding. The visions that I saw told me that as intelligent beings from all over our universe reaches the required perfection and metamorphose into pure energy as what happened to Jesus, so does our universe expand. With Einstein's equation: energy equals mass multiplied by the speed of light squared, you can imagine the massive energy created by just the body of Jesus converting into pure energy to be one with the Supreme Power Above us. I saw that we intelligent beings have these choices: aim for perfection and metamorphose body and soul to be one with the SPA in eternal life or be evil and your life is terminated, the residual energy of your consciousness or soul becomes the Higgs-Boson particle responsible for the formation of physical matter and I saw this occurring in the magma chamber of earth that oozes out as lava, called the lake of fire in the Bible, lava cools down to become rock that erodes to dust, the dirt of the earth, no more reasoning, no more thinking, dead forever. There is a ten-thousand-year-old Hindu belief that the lowest form you can come back is as a rock, which agrees with the visions I saw. Therefore, someone ten thousand years ago saw the same vision I saw. This is another proof that there is a Supreme Power Above guiding humanity from the dawn of civilization. We intelligent beings are the larvae of God. Just like a tree that produces seeds to propagate itself, our universe is continuously seeded with life for its expansion. Since the purpose of life is for the expansion of our Supreme Power Above, killing another human being is obviously an utmost offense to the purpose of our creation so that if you kill a human life, your life will be terminated as well.

Jesus told me that his words: you need to be born again, confirms the Buddhist belief in reincarnation and his letter to the church of Laodicea in the Revelation is for the Buddhists who are neither hot nor cold in enlightening humanity of the doctrine of reincarnation and Nirvana. In fact, when Jesus spoke about John, he said that he was Elijah who has come back, clearly implying reincarnation. When our physical body dies, our consciousness or soul continues to live if we are worthy of life and shall be born again to continue seeking perfection. I saw that all the innocent victims of the Holocaust and Islamic terrorisms are born again into glorious new lives. I saw all Nazis guilty of genocide and terrorists who are hailed as martyrs were all cast to the lake of fire dead forever to become the dirt of the earth.

There is a documentary on YouTube about near death experiences where men of science concluded that our consciousness or what is called the soul, is not dependent on our physical body for its survival after they witnessed those who were proclaimed clinically dead for as long as an hour but were resuscitated back to health with tales of reaching a beautiful place full of love but were told it was not their time. From these tales of people with near death experiences, it appears that heaven is an alternate universe from the physical universe that we experience while alive on earth. I know that they cannot enter heaven yet because they did not have their physical body converted to pure energy with them. I have heard testimonies from two people very dear and close to me about an out of body experience, where they saw their physical body still asleep while their consciousness was awake. Both experienced being very relieved when their soul or consciousness and physical body became one again in an instant.

Humanity has fallen deep in decadence and God has called on us to save humanity from doom before it is too late. After experiencing paranormal phenomenon that to me are miracles, I believe that the meteor that sent the dinosaurs to extinction was not an accident. I believe that the Supreme Power sent the dinosaurs to extinction after failing to evolve into intelligent beings after roaming on earth for 1.5 million years, to give mammals the chance to evolve into the intelligent beings that we are now. Please help me carry out this task God laid on my shoulders and save humanity before earth suffers another global extinction of species to start anew. I am sure that this pandemic that is plaguing humanity right now is a warning from God. Lava continuously flowed out of Mount Kilauea for over two decades since it erupted in 1983 and from the visions God showed me, they are the souls of the unredeemable sinners, such as vicious murderers, followers of the false prophet who killed those who do not believe them and Nazis guilty of genocide during the Holocaust that were cast unto the lake of fire.

There are signs observed by Geologists that the super volcano at Yellow Stone is swelling. I know that if sinners continuously get cast to the lake of fire, this super volcano will erupt and science already forecasted that if this happens, it will be the end of the United States of America and another global extinction of species because it will envelope earth with a cloud of dust that will prevent growth of food and all living creatures will starve to death. This is the exact vision that Nostradamus saw in his end of our world prophesy, which according to his interpreters, will happen in two decades. I implore you; God is calling on you through me. You can convey this message to all of humanity and I hope you will not decline God's summon. We must stop this end of our world prophesy of Nostradamus from happening. We must stop sinner souls turning into particle in lava that will make the Yellow Stone super volcano erupt. I am thinking that science thinks there is really nothing we can do about it that is why they are not making a big deal about this cataclysmic event that can happen because it is useless to create panic, but they say it can happen tomorrow or next century, they cannot tell. We must all aim for the perfection of Jesus to rapture or reach Nirvana before our world ends. Our solar system has about 5 billion years of life span left.

My first self-published book is titled The Book of life where I summoned everyone to sign in the book of life, but I wrote this book before the full magnitude of my task was revealed to me. It was the terrorist attack in New York City on that horrendous event of September 11, 2001 that I became aware of the enormity of the task on my shoulders. I was still a coward, fearful of facing ridicule and I was fearful of the harm that may come to me from those offended by the message of my book after I read what the false prophet prescribed for anyone who insults him, when I wrote my second book, Pure Gift The Second. These three books that I self-published, drained all my retirement savings, and until now they are unnoticed. I have another self-published book that I wrote when I finally found the courage to boldly claim that I am the witness Jesus said would come for him and I titled it – The Second Coming of Jesus.

Satan is doing everything to block the message of the Second Coming of Jesus from getting out to humanity because it is the key to open the door where we can cast him to perdition. The publisher of my third book abandoned me after I paid them thousands of dollars because they know they can't squeeze any more money from me because my entire savings had been wiped out. The telephone number and email address I have of them had been disconnected or invalid. I am not getting any sales report. I don't know if it is selling or not. I tried the number they have on the internet, still I get a response, the number is invalid, did they block my number from getting through? Amazon is selling my books but they refuse to deal with me because their authorized contact is my publisher. I realized that Amazon will not give you information if you are not the one they dealt with to get a book in their items to sell. Today, after a repeated run around, I finally got someone at Amazon to give me two telephone numbers of the publisher of my book, Agar Publishing, I called the two numbers, they were both wrong numbers. They were numbers of bookstores who had nothing to do with Agar Publishing. It was not Agar Publishing I dealt with to publish my book, it was Booktrail Agency. I am not a writer; I am a retired Architect who happened to be chosen by God to carry out this task. I cannot ask Amazon to stop selling my book even if someone else is getting all the sales money because my priority is to get my task carried out, to disseminate to humanity the message of the Second Coming of Jesus. I don't care if I am not getting my royalty as author. Now I am writing the fourth book and I am giving it the title: Pure Gift, the Second Coming of Jesus where I am merging my two books together, Pure Gift the Second and the Second Coming of Jesus. Once my final book – Pure Gift, The Second Coming of Jesus - is ready, then I'll tell Amazon to stop selling my first two books that they are selling, which are robbing me of my royalty as author.

I challenge science, how did it happen that I was born to fulfill all the signs Jesus prophesied in his gospels? I am also a firsthand witness to manifestations of archetypes that emanated from our collective unconscious, exactly as what Dr. Carl Gustav Jung had perceived in his theory of the collective unconscious. Why is Dr. Carl Gustav Jung ignored completely? Is it because he was the psychoanalyst of the third Reich, a Nazi? It was the negative dynamic archetype that manifested to me on the last three months of 1975, created by destructive evil thoughts, false beliefs and superstitions, and the prevailing subject of devil possession which held the attention of man at that time caused by the popularity of the movie the Exorcist, which I perceived as Satan because I did not know about Dr. Jung's theory at that time. Satan tried to turn me into a senseless mass killer and when he failed, he tried to kill me, but God saved me because I have this task to carry out. My ordeal with Satan was like being swallowed by an evil dragon to fulfill my sign of Jonah as prophesied by Jesus.

Mankind has been writing about manifestations of archetypes ever since man had learned to write, many written down as manifestation of God that interfered with their activities, as what Dr. Jung had stated, such as the god who told the children of Israel to kill everything that breathes in the land of their inheritance and the archetypal god that emanated from the collective unconscious of the people of Ballam who believed in sacrificing humans to please their god, who told Abraham to kill his son as sacrifice. God clearly told me that he will never contradict his law – DO NOT KILL. From my own personal experience, I believe there is a Supreme Power above who has been guiding humanity's evolution from its very beginning of existence. I believe I experienced what Moses and Buddha experienced. I believe that Pharaoh Akhenaten also had a God experience that made him drastically change the ancient polytheistic religion of Egypt to monotheism but because of the limited knowledge of man about our universe during his time, he perceived the one God as the Sun god. An Egyptian clergy must have correctly perceived that we need our physical body to reach the ultimate purpose of life and they responded with mummification.

Jesus unveiled the identity of the false prophet dressed in sheep's clothing but is a ravenous wolf. Followers of this false prophet focus only on his good words, mostly reiterations of the words of Jesus, but his violent words, which is leading his people to violate God's law – DO NOT KILL, is the most grievous offense to the purpose of our creation. The laws of life, handed down to us by Moses as the Commandments of God, all really boil down to DO NOT KILL, violating any of them causes conflicts or emotional distress that weakens the immune system that makes one susceptible to diseases that can kill. These laws of life are intended to keep us alive until we reach perfection to be one with the Supreme Power Above or in Buddhist terminology, to reach Nirvana. The Commandment – Thou keep holy the Sabbath day – is interpreted by all organized religions as – go to church. God is not a vain God who needs worship and praises. God dwells not in temples made by hand. Jesus said: You do not need to go to the synagogues to pray, pray in secret. Organized religions want us to go to church because they live on the donations that we give them. God told me that all that is expected from us is to seek for the ultimate purpose of life, to metamorphose body and soul to be one with God in eternal life in the alternate universe that we call heaven or to reach Nirvana.

The horrendous September 11, 2001, terrorist attack in New York, aroused my curiosity about Islam. From a book about Islam and a supposedly best English translation of the Quran, 2 books borrowed from the city library, I learned that Muslims are worshipping the god who told Abraham to kill his son as burnt offering, an archetypal god that requires human sacrifice, which is written on Genesis chapter 22; verse 2, obviously a repeated pattern of the number 2. This verse was written more than three thousand years ago, but it clearly has the sign of the second coming of Jesus already, evidence of the work of the SPA.

As I read the Quran and I came to the violent words of Mohammad, *- smite the neck of infidels, take them for ransom, hooks awaits them, show no mercy to your enemies, -* I was stunned because they are the exact words that the terrorists are following, clear contradictions to the forgiving, loving words of Jesus. Suddenly, Jesus was beside me, telling me, "Beware of the false prophet dressed in sheep's clothing but is a ravenous wolf." I was in great terror because the Quran prescribed what should be done to one who insults Muhammad, I knew the harm that can befall me and my loved ones if I speak to anyone about this. When this was happening, I became aware that I was no longer on the 21st century earth, it looked to me that I was suddenly transported back to the time when Jesus walked on earth, I saw huge boulders, I was on a beach which must have been the beach of the sea of Galilee, I saw the young clean, neat looking Jesus with a beautiful blue sky behind him and I felt that I was speaking to my son. Is this a memory in my subconscious that came out from buried deep in my past incarnation? Trembling in fear, I told Jesus, "I Can't do this!" But then, I saw the dejected Jesus, his shoulders drooped in disappointment, saying, "You are the chosen one to do this." Then I knew I cannot say no to him, I must carry out this task laid on my shoulders and suddenly, I was back in my home on this 21st century.

When I started writing my book, I was still a coward, but that was two decades ago, I am no longer afraid of whatever would come, in fact a death threat already came to me from someone commenting on my Facebook page. I immediately went to the Police Department and gave them the manuscript of my Facebook page. I showed the Policeman the text on my cell phone from the terrorist showing my address, telling me that they know where to find me. I told the Police officer, "In case I suddenly get murdered, this is the reason why."

At the Kaaba, during the Haj of Islam, this archetypal god of the people of Balaam requiring human sacrifice is kept alive until today, worshipped by Muslims. God told me that the Quran was manmade. The false prophet poisoned the hearts of the children of Ismael to hate their brothers, the children of Isaac and unto this day, there is no true peace in the Middle East. I know exactly Satan's power of suggestion because I experienced it during my sign of Jonah ordeal. I rejected the evil suggestions of Satan because I knew it was not my own thought, it was Satan making me think of grabbing stabbing implements to kill everyone around me. If only both the Jews and the Muslims would realize that it is Satan continuously making them nurture thoughts of animosity between them that make them forget that they are brothers, both their ancestors, Isaac and Ismael, were sons of Abraham. They can start forgiving each other and truly love each other like true brothers should, there will be peach in the Middle East. The children of Isaac that evolved as Israel were already punished by the Babylonian, the Romans and the Nazis and when they took refuge in the land of their ancestors, instead of their brothers welcoming them, they had to wage a war against their own brother who rejected to share the land of their ancestors with them. I know Satan's power of suggestion was again victorious. Satan wants the Muslims and the Jews to keep killing each other so that their souls will all become a particle in the magma chamber of earth that oozes out as lava to prevent them from reaching perfection that will turn their bodies into pure energy to be one with God. God told me that the children of Ismael are the prodigal sons of Abraham, and a big banquet awaits them upon their return to the true faith.

After my disappointment that my books are still unnoticed, I decided to accept all Facebook friend requests that are coming to me by the hundreds daily to carry out this task laid by God on my shoulders. I am now interacting with 3.5 thousand of them. One of them told me: He is Muslim and a messenger told us that the Jews are the worst of iniquity, they make corruption in the earth. Once again, I knew that this is another Satan's suggestions to the minds of Muslims. I know that it can feel that you are responsible for such evil thoughts but since I have never entertained evil thoughts, I rejected it and that was how I realized how Satan can take over one's consciousness. I told this Muslim Facebook friend that it is Satan making this evil suggestion to you to prevent you from having peace with your own brothers, he immediately became unavailable. I saw on the PBS channel the current happenings at the Middle East between the Jews and the Muslims. I pray that they both would open their eyes to the truth instead of listening to the evil urgings of Satan.

When the Romans embraced Christianity, the belief system that they propagated was intertwined with pagan Roman worship rituals. They continued carving and painting images of deities replacing Jupiter with the image of Jesus with a golden crown, ignoring what Jesus said – give up your material possessions. I was a sophomore student in high school who was in my World History class that was on the Roman history part of the lesson, when there was an unexpected vision that flashed in my mind. It was a vision of Jupiter with a golden crown seated on his throne and suddenly I saw him cast out up in space vanished and replaced by Jesus with a golden crown on his head. I was stupefied, wondering what that vision was about but I immediately went back to pay attention to my teacher's lessons. Now I see that God had been speaking to me since I was a child. Now that I see that the early Roman Christians replaced Jupiter with Jesus, Juno with Mary and the minor pagan gods with the Saints. They edited the first Commandment, Exodus 20;4, and deleted the edict that forbids images. God showed me that the Original first Commandment handed down to Moses clearly forbids worshipping images from the heaven, earth and seas. The early Roman Christians edited the first Commanded to what was acceptable to their ideology which was still very much influenced by their pagan tradition of worshipping a humanoid god. They continued their litanies evolving into the rosary, ignoring the words of Jesus, do not say repeated prayers. The bejeweled garb of the high Roman priest became the attire of the Pope. This is the beginning of the Roman Catholic church. Greco-Roman literature is laden with apparition of deities because these apparitions are the direct result of idolatry and repeated prayers. Apparitions of deities are visual manifestations of archetypes emanating from our collective unconscious created by collective beliefs, as what Dr. Carl Gustav Jung had perceived.

The pagan Romans did not believe in reincarnation, so they interpreted the words of Jesus – You need to be born again – as convert to a Christian way of life, this is the doctrine that was propagated all throughout Christianity. Jesus did not say convert, Jesus said you need to be born again. When the words of Jesus floated out of the pages of the Bible when he was asked if to be born again meant, to be in a mother's womb and born as a baby, and his response was vague and unclear, I asked God why, and I saw images of how human's early response to reincarnation was the caste system where men were not born equal, one born as a serf, is a serf for life and has no chance to get to a higher level of social rank. I understood. Now God made it clear to me that reincarnation means that if you are worthy of life, when your physical body dies, your consciousness or soul, will be reincarnated into a new life as a baby, to continue seeking for perfection to attain the ultimate purpose of life, to rapture body and soul to be one with God in eternal life.

Martin Luther and his followers protested the materialistic and inhumane abuses of the Catholics, and they did away with some idolatry while they continued to worship Jesus as god keeping the Cross as sign of Christianity and the Protestant Church came about, they continued to completely ignore Revelation 22;9 where Jesus told John not to worship him because he is his fellow servant. They preached salvation by faith alone, that they will go straight to heaven when they die, ignoring John 3;13 that says, no one has ascended to heaven except he who came down from heaven, which to my perception, means only Jesus has ascended to heaven. No dead human gets to heaven. You need to be alive to Rapture or reach Nirvana to get to heaven. That's why in Revelation 21:4 it says there shall be no more death. We don't leave lifeless cadavers anymore when we Rapture or reach Nirvana.

Early Christians did not worship Jesus as God and they called him the good shepherd; thus, the Protestants called their priests Pastors. They preach that you do not have to be perfect because the blood of Jesus saved you already which is blasphemy because Jesus clearly said, you need to be perfect as God in heaven is perfect. Both Catholics and Protestants engaged in bloody wars, both failed to reject Satan's suggestions of animosity between them, completely oblivious of God's law – DO NOT KILL. I am sure they were all cast to the lake of fire. This is happening again in this present time between the Jews and Muslims.

My friend tried to recruit me to join her Presbyterian Church, so I told her that I need to speak to her Pastor. Pastor Evans was so nice to visit me at my home. I told him that I witnessed the second coming of Jesus and I told him that Jesus said, "Do not worship me, worship God in heaven," and about the false gods who are Satan in disguise in the Old Testament who told man to kill, Genesis 22;2 and Deuteronomy 20;16. He told me that if I cannot accept that Jesus is God and the Bible is 100% the words of God, I cannot join his Church. I went to see other Catholic Priests and other Protestant Pastors; they all rejected me. The only clergy that gave me an encouraging hug and approval was an elderly retired Priest of the Anglican church, but his young replacement Priest obviously did not want him to give me more attention and quickly pulled him away from me. God himself showed me that the gods in the Bible telling people to kill were Satan in disguise, and Jesus himself told me not to worship him, how can I accept that the Bible is 100% the words of God? Jesus consoled me when he said, "You do not need to go to the Synagogue to pray, pray in secret."

Although Jesus confirmed that the Buddhist belief in reincarnation is true, Buddhism is also flawed with superstitious worship rituals. All organized religions on earth are flawed with false beliefs. All belief systems of all organized religions still being followed today were formulated when the intellect of man was still in its lower stage of evolution, and they are all affected by manifestations of archetypes created by collective false beliefs of early man. Religion is supposed to bring peace to earth but today, in our age of information, it is still the root cause of conflicts and wars. Jesus said, if salt has lost its savor, it is good for nothing but to be trampled by the foot of man. In this age of information, It is time to acknowledge and eradicate all false beliefs to unify all of humanity' beliefs based on absolute scientific truths to end all wars.

I am the witness attesting to the fact that Jesus made his promised second coming, he appeared to me, and only the words of Jesus and the Commandments handed down to us by Moses are the words of the true God. Christians lay their hands on the Bible when they make vows, believing that the Bible is 100% the words of God. God told me that it is now the end time for false beliefs. All the signs of this end time for all man-made dogmas are upon us, the Covid plague, wars and rumors of wars, nations against nations vying to outdo each other in producing nuclear weapons for mass destruction which will surely destroy our world. What good are these weapons of mass destruction? Why should we destroy our world? Please help me awaken these nations that are aspiring to outdo each other in developing the most lethal nuclear weapon of mass destruction that will annihilate humanity. I am sure that a few will survive if ever a third world war breaks out, which will surely be a catastrophic nuclear war, but it will take a longer time to attain the ultimate purpose of life. Our solar system has only about five billion years left before it dies, we must evolve to perfection to be one with the Supreme Power Above before this happens.

After receiving all these revelations from God, I now see that Lucifer and Satan are so delighted watching us kill each other like ferocious animals. Lucifer and Satan are anti-life because the ultimate purpose of life is to turn physical matter into pure energy to be one with God. Lucifer and Satan are behind all human sacrificing religions because they want all intelligent beings to be evil because the residual energy of an evil soul or consciousness upon the demise of the physical body becomes a particle in physical matter that will maintain this physical universe. Are black holes that are devouring physical matters processing physical matters into pure energy to be transmitted back to the alternate universe we call heaven, where Lucifer fell out from? If it is, it is not sentient energy, unlike when humans Raptures to be pure sentient energy.

The story of Cain and Abel tells us that we are the descendants of Cain who slaughtered his own brother Abel out of jealousy because his material offerings were rejected by God while Abel's offerings were accepted by god. The truth is that Cain was worshipping the true God who do not need material offerings and Abel's god was an archtypal god requiring offerings and we must eradicate all false gods. It was through this myth that God told me that worshipping is not God's requirement. Only a man-made god can accept material offerings and outward show of piety. Jesus said that you do not need to go to a synagogue to pray. Are these the words that threatened the Rabbis that they denounced Jesus as disturbing the peace that led to his crucifixion? Jesus said that it is better to pray in secret. Worshipping is not a requirement of God but a need of man. If you need to join a church to be part of a social organization, go, but God bids us to unify our beliefs so that we would reach peace on earth.

God walked me through the Commandments. The Commandments of God handed down to us by Moses are in fact the laws of life, follow them and you will reach the promised immortality of your life, defy them and your life will be terminated, and the residual energy of your soul shall become a particle, which to me is what the Higgs-Boson particle is, that is responsible for the formation of physical matter. These laws of life aim to promote harmonious human relationships. Those who adhere to superstitions and false beliefs will not attain purity of mind to reach perfection. When these laws of life are defied, emotional distress results to those who are directly affected by such defiance to these laws. Emotional distress lowers the immune system of our body which makes us vulnerable to diseases that can cause death, which is contrary to the purpose of our creation. All these Commandments, in fact boil down to DO NOT KILL.

God said, "*Thou shall not have graven images before me.*" Any symbolism that identifies one religion from another is a violation to this Commandment. The cross, the image of Jesus, the image of Mary, the image of Buddha, the image of any kind of deity, the menorah, the Star of David, head scarves, domes, or any object or writing that is used to symbolize a belief system is a violation to God's Commandment. Exodus 20;4 clearly commands us not to have any images or any likeness to anything that is in heaven above, or that is in the earth beneath, or that is in the water under the earth. Anyone who does not believe that there is any relevance to this Commandment is blind to see that the turmoil caused by differences of religious beliefs are preventing us from reaching peace on earth. God wants none of these symbolisms. Jesus said, *"Do not worship me, worship God in heaven."* It was the Council of Nicaea, whose judgement was very much influenced by their previous beliefs of worshipping a humanoid god and their pagan worship rituals, which decided that Jesus is God, the world power those days were the Roman Empire. Emperor Constantine accepted Christianity after he saw a vision telling him that he would win his war if he fought under the emblem of the Christian cross. He did win his wars, so he accepted Christianity, but the pagan Roman religion and their pagan worship rituals still very much influenced his way of thinking, as well as all other Romans of that time. They interpreted the first Commandment as, that images of Jesus and those related to him are not graven images. Anyone who worships Jesus as God is violating this Commandment. In this age of information, we know that Earth is an insignificant dot that is hardly visible viewing our entire physical universe. How can a man be the Supreme Power of this vast universe?

"Do not take the name of God in vain." God said through Moses that whosoever takes the name of God in vain is not guiltless. Followers of the false prophet who profess the name of this false prophet as the prophet of God are guilty of violating this commandment because to profess the name of the false prophet as a prophet of God is taking the name of God in vain. Those who say that the god who told Abraham to kill his son is really God is taking the name of God in vain and they too are guilty of violating this Commandment. God showed me in a vision that those who preach that the god in Deuteronomy 20;16 who told the children of Israel to go to the land of their inheritance and kill everything

that breathes, was an archetypal god from their belief that they were the chosen people. To proclaim that the Bible, old and new testaments, as 100% the word of God is taking God's name in vain. Many stories in the Old Testament were adaptations from the Book of Gilgamesh, the story of the great flood included, written before the Torah. Those who take God's name in vain are guilty because they are fueling brain wave energies that embolden the commission of killing people of a different faith by those who are falsely made to believe that such is what God wants them to do.

"Remember to keep holy every seventh day." Keep your body whole and not broken up with ailments. God bids us to take a break from work so that we will not get burnt up from exhaustion. This Commandment is for us to keep our body healthy because the purpose of our lives is to reach immortality, which is not possible without healthy bodies. Do not ingest anything that will kill you, no harmful drugs, no excessive alcohol, no excessive food, that is why gluttony is a sin because it leads to obesity that leads to more ailments. Everyone should be aware of toxins in food preservatives, hair dyes, tattoo inks, make ups that are absorbed by the skin and carried by blood stream to various body organs that can cause ailments. Jesus said, *"Man does not live by bread alone but by every word of God"*. The wage of sin is death because sin makes the body produce death agents or free radicals that weakens our immune system and makes us vulnerable to diseases that can kill us. It is true that we must learn to avoid all cardinal sins, or negative emotions, to help bolster the efficiency of our immune system in fighting off diseases. In conjunction to this, it is imperative that we keep our world free of pollutions that will hinder our quest for immortality.

The words of Jesus, *"Upon this rock I shall build my church,"* was meant for his people two thousand years ago. Jesus needed his disciples to preach the words of God because during his time there were no schools. Now in our generation, all schools in every nation must teach History of Religion to every child of our world so that they will learn all the good and the bad that all different belief systems had brought to humanity. It is time to enlighten all of humanity of the profoundness of Dr. Carl Gustav Jung's theory of the collective unconscious. Let us rectify the erroneous deeds of those who took away God from schools and who took away the Commandments of God carved in stone in government edifices.

"Honor thy father and thy mother." It is wrong to say you did not ask to be born. You chose to be born of your parents to learn whatever lessons you need to learn from them to atone for whatever transgressions you committed in your past life. Your parents may be rewards from heaven for a life well lived in your past incarnation. If you happen to have negligent parents, you are atoning for your past life of being a negligent parent to your children as well. What you do unto others shall be done unto you. Many negligent parents produce children that become criminals. This shows how being a negligent parent can get one cast to the lake of fire.

"Do not kill." God showed me that it was a manmade god who bade the children of Israel to commit genocide, wiping out six tribes, killing babies and little children, the aged, and even their animals. Unto this day, there are Jews who boldly claim Palestinian land crying out, "This is our God-given right!" Thus: the Babylonians, the Romans and the Nazi's tried to annihilate the Jews as well because what you do unto others shall be done unto you. God clearly showed me that any god who tell his people to kill are man-made gods. God showed me that the god of the children of Israel who bade them to go the cities of their inheritance and kill everything that breathes was an archetypal god created by their collective beliefs that they were favored by god so they believed they can slaughter anyone on their way. Those who execute innocent people in the name of a false god have chosen to burn in the lake of fire and if your sincerest contrition delivers you from the lake of fire you would still be born again into a life of hell on earth, but at least you are still alive and have the chance to redeem yourself.

You cannot kill for whatever reason except self-defense. Even in self-defense, once a person had killed another human being, his physical life would surely end in death because the guilt will prevent him from reaching immortality, but his soul has a chance to reincarnate. When you kill in self-defense you save your assailant from being cast unto the lake of fire. Anyone who does not repent for a grievous transgression has chosen to terminate his or her life program and will surely burn in the lake of fire. God is merciful for those who ask for mercy, but the law of creation stands; what you do unto others shall be done unto you.

Jesus preached forgive, turn your other cheek, give your coat as well if someone takes your jacket, love your enemy, because doing so prevents you from becoming a killer. Killing will surely kill you permanently body and soul. If you kill yourself, you will be trapped in a non-ending cycle of being born again and committing suicide over and over until you become a suicide bomber killing others, then you are surely dead forever. If you are suicidal, snap out of it, seek for professional help if you cannot find solace in seeking for God. Executing a convicted criminal is a form of self-defense as well as killing an enemy at war. If you execute a murderer criminal, you have given that criminal a chance to be born again and you can expect great bloodshed because they will be born to kill. Such is what happened to Adam Lanza who was a mass killer in Sandy Hook Elementary School as well as the senseless killing perpetrated by Ethan Crumbley. If you spare his life for his crimes and imprison him for life, it is the criminal alone who can redeem himself depending on how truly contrite he or she is for whatever crime he or she committed. Let the criminal die a natural death and if he is unrepentant, he will surely be cast to the lake of fire. Repeal the death penalty. This is why God said, DO NOT KILL.

There is a great outrage for the wrongful death of a criminal from the knees of a mindless policeman. In truth, this policeman had given the criminal, who had chosen the path towards the lake of fire, attested by his lengthy record of crimes he had committed, every chance to be born again. Now, this mindless policeman is facing the path towards the lake of fire if he does not sincerely repent for his misdeed.

Even the act of bigotry can kill your soul. If you feel you are being discriminated because of your race, it means that you were a racist bigot in your past life and if you cannot endure the discrimination you are getting, and resort to violence, then you can see how bigotry can send one to the lake of fire. Those who are protesting racial discrimination are the bigots in their past life, born again unto the race they despised and if they resort to murder to loudly display their protest, they are headed for the death of their souls, to burn in the lake of fire. Even if your act of sincere contrition prevents the death of your soul whatever you did to another will be done unto you either in this life or the next. Don't ever think that you can get away with murder because you will definitely be cast to hell fire because an act of contrition is not sincere if there was no admission to the crime committed to ease the pain of the survivors of your victim or victims.

If you have committed a perfect murder, your choice is to burn in the lake of fire after the demise of your physical body to be dead forever or admit to your crime to give closure to the grieving loved ones of your murder victim and make a most sincere act of contrition. But even if you are given a chance to be born again, you will be born again in hell right here on earth. If you feel you are having a hellish life, it means you are atoning for your grave misdeeds in your past life. You have the choice to redeem yourself or be cast to the lake of fire. What you do unto others shall be done unto you. If you are going through severe depression, ask yourself, are you depressed because of unfulfilled desires? This is the reason Jesus said put yourself last. Your depression may be caused by your own selfishness. Focus on what you can do for others instead, to get out of your depression.

Abortion is the killing of a human fetus and therefore diminishes respect for human life. Someone argued that a fetus is not human life, what kind of life is it then? A human fetus has human DNA and therefore it is human. Some would argue that disallowing abortion is against a woman's civil rights. If we consider Dr. Carl Gustav Jung's theory of the collective unconscious, what would the consequence be for a diminished respect for human life in the collective unconscious of the human race? This will boost the negative dynamic archetype in its pursuit to terminate human life, thus a murderer's chore to kill will be done with much more ease.

Which is more important to you, would you give more consideration for the human right of a woman who seeks to terminate her growing human fetus in her womb, or would you be more concerned about the victims of murders because the chore to commit murder has been given more ease because of the diminished respect for life? Abortion must be stopped all together because abortion is killing a human life and is a factor for the termination of more lives, proponents of abortion are all not guiltless of the deaths of innocent victims of senseless killings since they diminished respect for life that made it easier for the senseless killer to commit his senseless act. If a woman does not want to get pregnant, with the present-day knowledge of birth control, there is no more excuse for abortion. If a woman gets pregnant because of rape, it is a cross the victim must bear, she must give birth to the baby and have the baby adopted by willing adoptive parents to uphold respect for life. I know prostitutes go to hell. Rape is hell. To be raped as a child is worse hell. In a vision, I saw that prostitutes and adulterers of low morals behaving like lowly animals, that escaped the lake of fire, will be born again to be the target of rapists who are also behaving like lowly animals. This is again another issue of Karma or what you do unto others shall be done unto you. In a vision I saw that people who behave like lowly animals do not deserve intelligent life and if they escape the lake of fire, they will be born again as lowly animals.

The earthly pleasures derived from the act of procreation is the reward for creating life. Proponents of abortion demand the reward but shun the purpose that warrants that reward. The act of sexual intercourse should be kept sacred and not just taken casually for physical pleasure. Both man and woman share the responsibility of the procreation of human life from reckless sexual intercourse. If you are not ready to procreate, you better give a lot of thought into having sexual intercourse before you jump into it. This is why we have the law of life, DO NOT KILL. If your pregnancy is endangering your life then terminating your pregnancy is self-defense but if you did not take all the necessary precautions to avoid pregnancy and commit abortion you will have to do a lot of atonement to avoid the hell fire. Since committing abortion guarantees your future physical death, it is your choice to make, to give the fetus in your womb a chance to live and hope you will survive its delivery otherwise, you reincarnate sooner and have the chance to rapture body and soul sooner.

"*Do not commit Adultery.*" Cheating your partner is not a sin that will bring you to lake of fire, but any sin will forfeit your chance to reach immortality. You will die for sure and when you get born again the temptation to commit a more grievous sin will be greater. Polygamous men and women are guilty. I am a firsthand witness to the deep anguish a wife suffers from the infidelity of her spouse. Cheaters of any relationship are guilty whether there is marriage or not. Rape is a horrendous transgression that can lead one to toast in the lake of fire.

"*Do not steal.*" Not only do you hurt the person you stole from, but you will also be deprived of finding true happiness because true happiness can only be attained with a completely clear conscience free of any wrongdoing towards anyone. Return what you stole and make amends for your crime, otherwise, you will be tormented with guilt and emptiness within you for the rest of your life. True happiness is in giving not in taking. Corruption is stealing. You cannot take anything that is not rightfully yours and bribes are among them as well as whatever you get from extortion. All corrupt government officials who accept or demand bribes or steal funds intended for the development of the country are guilty. Corporate magnates who do not fairly share company profits with everyone who has invested their efforts to acquire these profits are guilty, there must be fair profit sharing to all employees if one does not want to face the consequence of stealing. Greed is the motivating factor to violate this Commandment and for as long as you have greed in your heart you will not reach the true happiness that will bring everlasting life. Those who amassed great wealth because of greed and corruption shall be born again in dire poverty, to suffer the effects of their greed and corruption. Sloth is one of the cardinal sins because you have stolen the energy of the benevolent one who did the work for you that you did not do because of your laziness.

"*Do not bear false witness.*" Teaching false doctrines is a violation of this Commandment. Teaching the doctrines of the false prophet is bearing false witness and if your teaching led someone to kill, your soul is in grave danger. Teaching that God gave the specifications for a place of worship, or an object of worship is bearing false witness. God dwells not on temples made by hand. Teaching that Jesus is God is bearing false witness, Jesus said, do not worship me. Refusing to accept that man evolved from the lower animals is bearing false witness. Proclaiming that the white race is superior to other races on earth is bearing false witness, our souls do not have race, we are all children of God, you can be white today and be born again black in your next incarnation. White skin is more vulnerable from the harmful effects of ultraviolet rays that causes skin cancer whereas the darker pigmentation of human skin is more resistant to UV rays. Refusing to admit that man is responsible for the raising level of carbon dioxide in our atmosphere and saying that it is the will of God alone that is causing global warming is bearing false witness. We have to keep our world free of pollution hazardous to our health to attain the ultimate goal of immortality. Teaching that homosexuals are an abomination to the eyes of God is bearing false witness. Jesus said some eunuchs are created in their mother's womb, what is the difference between a eunuch and a homosexual? God has no sex. If sex is still a big priority in your life, then you are not ready to go to heaven. You cannot get to heaven when earthly desires are still bogging you down. Jesus said do not judge. The real test is longevity. If statistics show that homosexuals have shorter life spans, then we would know it is really detrimental to one's health and it should be avoided since the purpose of life is to be immortal. God told me that it was a man-made god created by energies of brain waves of men who cannot give up the patriarchal role of man in society who manifested to the false prophets who promote polygamy and Joseph Smith is one of them. Therefore, teaching the doctrines that lead to polygamy and exploitation of women is bearing false witness. An impostor hacking the identity of another for felonious reasons is bearing false witness against the person he stole the Identity from.

Teaching the myth that Adam and Eve are the first humans on earth as the truth is bearing false witness. Scientific anthropological findings clearly show that we Homo sapiens evolved from the same ancestors of monkeys. The myth of Adam and Eve tells us of a serpent who told Eve that eating the fruit of knowledge will make you be like God. The message of the Second Coming of Jesus is that we must believe nothing but the absolute truth to be one with God. Adhering to false beliefs and superstitions prevents attaining purity of mind to become perfect to reach God. Ancient man must have vilified the message that eating the fruit of knowledge will make you be like God, so they portrayed the messenger as a lowly venomous serpent. Eve, a woman, was the one who plucked the fruit of knowledge and gave it to Adam. I am a woman, chosen by God to eradicate all false beliefs and to convey this message to humanity. It seems to me that this is the true significance of this myth.

"Do not covet your neighbor's goods." You must learn to draw energy from a higher source to inflate your depleted energy. If you insult or bully someone to make you feel better, you are guilty of violating this commandment because you took someone's energy to inflate yours. You cannot make someone feel bad so that you can feel better without any negative consequences. We must be considerate of each other's feelings.

"Do not covet your neighbor's wife or husband or partner." We must respect relationships. Anyone who knowingly entices a man or a woman who is already committed to another in a relationship is guilty regardless of whether there is marriage or not.

All these Commandments are guidelines for harmonious relationships among mankind and any violation will forfeit any hope for immortality. We are still in the process of evolving to a higher state of being. The more evolved a person is the easier it is to follow the Commandments. Believing false dogmas will hamper one's evolution to a higher state. The less evolved a person is, the closer that person is to the animal state of being. Homo sapiens are still animals. When a person reaches that state where he or she no longer commit sins then he or she has evolved into another specie that is truly the child of God and Homo

Domine sounds like a rightful name for that specie. It is still inherent in the psyche of Homo sapiens that to be materially affluent is a guarantee for survival because buried deep in the human psyche is the memory of the days when he was still a primitive hunter-gatherer where every day is a struggle to stay alive. We must break away from the effect of these primitive memories to advance in our evolution process because this memory is the root for the desire for material things. This is keeping us from breaking away from Homo sapiens to evolve into Homo Domine specie that will lead to immortality. This is the reason Jesus said give up all your material possessions, come and follow me. Jesus told us to forgive, to love your enemy, to turn your other cheek because another Homo sapiens characteristic that we need to break away from to evolve to a higher specie is vindictiveness. If you allow anyone to upset you, you are the loser because your body will produce the death agents that will weaken your immune system making you susceptible to diseases that can kill. We must learn to control our anger and learn to forgive. For as long as we seek for vengeance instead of forgiveness we will stay as animals still waging wars and killing each other just like lowly unintelligent animals who have no ability to negotiate for peace.

Jesus said, give up your material possession and when I followed this advice, I realized how exhilarating it feels to be freed from material want, no more worries that I will be robbed of my material possessions, no more worries that I will be mugged for precious jewels that I would have been wearing. I felt so free – Hallelujah! Now, when I see a bejeweled person, all I can feel for him or her is pity that he or she still needs these cumbersome trinkets to gain attention, acceptance, respect? I don't need them anymore. If everyone will only realize how much more comfortable life is without these bodily decorations, they will find the true inner peace that is the main ingredient for finding true happiness. Thirst for material things is unquenchable, the more you get, the more you want, and you will never get the satisfaction you clamor for.

Organized Religions are social organizations. If they ignore these messages of the second coming of Jesus and continue preaching what

Jesus called commandments of man, which are false beliefs and man-made dogmas, they will not attain purity of mind which is necessary to attain the perfection to rapture into pure energy to be one with God in eternal life. There were no schools during the time of Jesus two thousand years ago. When Jesus said, "upon this rock I shall build my church", it was meant for the people of his generation two thousand years ago. In this 21st century, humanity subjects in all schools should educate our children of the history of religions with the good and the bad effects it had on our intellectual evolution. The primary message of the second coming of Jesus is: Science is the absolute truth. What is the relevance of religion to our pursuit of scientific truth? All we need to do is to follow all the laws of life or Commandments of our Supreme Power Above, to reach the ultimate purpose of our lives.

I tried to disseminate these messages of God to us in the 21st century by blogging. I knew the new messages are politically incorrect, so I used my maiden name Pura Regalado as the blogger to avoid any negative repercussion to my loved ones. Facebook was just starting at that time, and I got an invitation from FB to join in and all I answered was yes and so my FB identity is Pura Regalado since them and my profile photo was taken at that time. While posting my blog, I was suddenly in awe, my eyes and mouth wide open, when I started typing words not coming from my mind, it was automatic writing. God must have chiseled His Commandments in stone using the hands of Moses just as God wrote His message to humanity through me using my fingers. Therefore, I believe I experienced what Moses experienced. Blog.com immediately isolated my blogs inaccessible to the public as soon as they noticed the political incorrectness of my blogs and I stopped blogging when I realized that the purpose for my blog can no longer be carried out.

Through my fingers, God wrote: *Peace on earth can only be attained if all organized religions will make these following peace offerings for world peace:*

The Jews shall sacrifice the god who told them to kill everything that breathes in the land of their inheritance and accept the words of Jesus as true words from God. Jesus said I came to uphold the Commandments not to break them confirming that the Commandments handed down to Moses were from the true God.

The Catholics, Greek Orthodox and Hindus shall sacrifice all idolatrous worship of religious sculptures and images and repeated prayers.

The Buddhists shall sacrifice their superstitious worship rituals.

The Moslems shall sacrifice their false prophet Mohammad and the manmade Quran.

All Christians shall sacrifice their god Jesus, their true sacrificial lamb. Jesus said do not worship me, worship God in heaven.

In the olden days, it would have been written like this: God bade Pura to open the Bible. What I experienced was a compelling urge to open the Bible. I was raised Catholic at a time when reading the Bible was not encouraged without clergy supervision to avoid interpretations contrary to theirs. I was not a Bible reader at all. All I knew were the Gospels that were read during Sunday masses before the sermon. I have never read the Old Testament before all these miraculous experiences. I did not know who Abraham was.

As soon as I held the Bible on my hands, it miraculously opened to the pages that God wanted me to read, and the texts floated out of the page and were magnified a hundred-fold with vivid visions showing me what they meant. The sensation I felt was that of hearing the voice of Jesus and not reading it. If God did not open the Bible for me to the exact pages I was supposed to read, I would not know what to look for and where to find them. While I was going through my sign of Jonah ordeal, I opened the Bible in the Revelation and read it all aloud to counter the demonic suggestions that were coming to my mind. Two decades later, in one of my travels, I came upon a Bible in a hotel room that started the Revelation with: Blessed is the one who reads aloud the words of this prophesy, and blessed are those who hear it and take to heart what is written in it, because the time is near. I was astounded, my Bible has no mention of reading it aloud. Indeed, I read the Revelation aloud and the truth were revealed to me. In Revelation, it says – and death shall be no more - because when we reach the perfection of Jesus, or Nirvana, we don't leave any more lifeless cadavers.

The opening of seals in the Revelation are scientific break-through discoveries of men that widened our understanding of how things are in the world we live in.

The visions I saw as the texts floated out of the pages of the Bible that miraculously opened to Christ's messages to the Churches are these:

The Church of Ephesus, I saw images of the Protestant church, which had left its first love, their search for the truth, and they settled with salvation by faith alone.

The Church of Smyrna, I saw images of the Seventh Day Adventist church, where the false prophet David Koresh evolved from.

The Church in Pergamos, I saw images of Islam, who holds the doctrine of Balaam, the doctrine of human sacrifice. Satan's seat is the seat of the false prophet Mohammad with his man-made Quran, who are leading them to violate God's commandment, DO NOT KILL. Right after this letter of Jesus to the church in Pergamos, it is written: *He that hath an ear, let him hear what the spirit saith unto the churches. To one who overcometh will I give to eat of the hidden manna and a white stone with a new name, which no man knoweth save the one who receiveth it.* God revealed

Pura whitestone

to me the ultimate purpose of life that I imparted to you, and I have the white stone with the letters SPA naturally scribed in it. SPA is for Supreme Power Above. The photograph of this white stone is on this book.

The Church in Thy-a-tira, I saw the images of the Catholic Church. I was a Catholic, I couldn't understand it at first until all the sex scandals of the church came out.

The Church in Sardis, I saw images of the Jehovah witnesses, they have a name for God, but God has no name. Was Jehovah the archetypal god who commanded the children of Israel to kill everything that breathes in the land of their inheritance? They refuse to use modern discoveries to prolong life which is contrary to the purpose of life.

The Church in Philadelphia, I saw images of Jewish synagogues, Jesus set an open door for them but until now they refuse to enter.

The Church in Load-i-cea, I saw images of Buddhists temples, which is neither cold nor hot in disseminating the truth about reincarnation and Nirvana.

Today we have the Covid plague. Atheism had taken away belief in God and men are falling to decadence, not taking the path towards the ultimate purpose of life. God told me that we are now on the end times, but it is a choice between the end of our world, or the end of false beliefs and man-made dogmas. Signs of the times are all here, are they not? Wars and rumors of wars, the plague, country vying against each other in producing weapons of mass destruction that will definitely bring an end to our world. We better wake up before it is too late. If we do nothing to prevent the end of the world prophesy of Nostradamus, then it is our loss.

God sent me to save all Muslims. Compare my signs from God from that of Mohammad's if he had any. Where in the Bible did Jesus say, one named Mohammad will come after me? Mohammad claimed that he was the seal of prophets. I am living proof of his lie. I am living proof that there is indeed God.

As a young woman, I never had intentions of leaving the place of my birth, but I don't think I would have fully understood the task that God laid on my shoulders if I did not come to the United States where my understanding of our universe widened up. The rest of my story is about who I am and the events that lead to my coming to America.

CHAPTER 2

The Sign of Jonah

Jesus said that the only sign that shall be given to an adulterous and evil generation is the sign of Jonah and indeed our generation is evil and adulterous. Jesus made me aware that I have the sign of Jonah. I had been swallowed by a dragon and I was in this dragon's belly for three months but it failed to digest me and it threw me out from its belly, back to my freedom after a horrifying three months of torture to carry out this most important task.

In the last three months of the year 1975, I had a most horrifying encounter with a vile energy that nobody else could feel except me. Twenty two years later, someone pointed out to me that 1975 also had the pattern of 2 because 1+9+7+5=22. In 1975, I was not aware yet that my life had the recurring pattern of the 2. It was exactly twenty two years later that I became aware of it because of my encounter with Jesus. I felt this demonic force attempting to overcome my reasoning to control my actions. Every time a pointed or sharp implement came to my sight, this evil force compelled me to stab everyone around me. It was so horrifying because it felt that the compulsion to kill was coming from my own mind but I knew in my heart that it was a foreign energy that was trying to possess me. It was so compelling but I knew I had to fight against it with all my might. Fortunately for me, I was raised to have very strong high moral values. Had I been morally bankrupt like many people today, this nefarious energy would have easily controlled me and I would have easily killed senselessly.

I was a faculty member at that time at the School of Architecture and Planning at MIT (Mapua Institute of Technology), Philippines. At that time in my life, I had become a skeptic who questioned the validity of metaphysical phenomena. I started to ask if God truly created man or if man created god. "If there really are metaphysical forces, let it manifest to me," I challenged. Much to my surprise and consternation, a force beyond my comprehension manifested to me and I was caught completely unprepared.

I am an Architect and at that time the Dean, Obi Mapua, the grandson of the school founder, was a very good friend of mine, we had a singing quartet that sang Peter Paul and Mary songs when we were students, and he invited me to teach Architectural subjects. He was confident that I would do well as an Instructor because as an Architectural student at MIT, I was top ranking, in fact I was the only scholar during my senior year. I earned my scholarship from my performance which based on the marks that I got was considered outstanding by my instructors in all my Architectural subjects as well as related engineering subjects. Aside from my B.S. degree in Architecture, I had earned teaching credits from EARIST (Eulogio Amang Rodriguez Institute of Science and Technology, my high school alma mater) plus I was in the process of earning my Master's degree from the University of the Philippines at that time, so I was fully qualified to be a member of the Faculty.

I was brought up as a devout catholic. In my teenage years, I was a member of a sisterhood, the Legion of Mary and sister Olive introduced me to a little book, The Imitation of Christ, and this little book had become my daily companion in my youth but higher college education made me question my religious beliefs, considering the scientific facts that I learned in physics and the sciences. However, although I had become a skeptic, my relationship with Jesus continued strong because his philosophy of life gave me peace within. When my encounter with this satanic energy that was compelling me to become a murderer grew formidable there was no one else to turn to but back to God's protective hands and I begged for his forgiveness for becoming doubtful. In my desperation I fervently implored for God's deliverance from this satanic force that was compelling me to kill senselessly. My students were in great danger if I failed. I had to stay away from them. I also had to abandon my quest for a master's degree in Architecture because my classmates would also be in mortal danger if this satanic force overcame me. Lucky for me at that time, I had four live-in domestic helpers, Naning, Marilyn, Tessie and Nara, who alternated as a cook, a laundry girl, a house cleaner, and they all took turns as nannies to my three children so I could stay away from the knives at the kitchen.

I had a Bible in my book shelf which I bought from the book store out of curiosity but I never had the chance to open it. At that desperate moment when I needed God's help to deliver me from this satanic force, when my mind was in desperate need for an answer to "Why are all these horrendous compulsions happening?" I took the Bible and opened it for the first time. It opened to the page where I read, "Thou shalt not invoke spirits". "I'm so sorry, I did not know I wasn't supposed to invoke spirits", as I prayed in deep contrition. It was so strange that the book opened exactly on the page where my eyes gazed directly on the passages that gave me the strength to fight off this nefarious force. I had never read the Bible before and I would never have known where to look for the right words that had given me the strength to fight. I did not have to search because my eyes went directly on the exact verses that were answering my questions and gave me strength. More strange was the fact that the biblical texts floated out of the page and was magnified twenty fold or more while vivid images came to my vision telling me what the words on the Bible meant. I was getting confused because some of the images that were coming forth were not in agreement with the teachings of the Catholic Church. There were moments when I was lost. I started asking, are these visions from God or are they deceiving me? I did not know what to do.

I had been going to bed at night holding the Bible on my chest because I felt that when my hands were on the Bible, the energy that was compelling me to reach for the knife was neutralized. Early one morning, after a sleepless night, I got up. With both my legs stretched on my bed, I laid the Bible on my knees and raised both my hands to push my hair away from my face when suddenly both my arms were no longer in my control. This was how I experienced the alien hand syndrome. Both my hands slid down from my face across to my neck and they started to strangle me. It was completely an alien force controlling both my hands strangling me but I did not have time to be fearful. I learned earlier that my fear fueled the strength of this evil energy. I was defiant and mentally fought with all my might against this nefarious energy that finally took control of my two hands. I defiantly proclaimed that Satan has no power over me because I am not an evil person and I am fully protected by God. I was raised a Catholic so I started reciting the Creed and as soon as I uttered the words I believe in God, the demonic force freed my hands and they were back in my control.

I hurriedly got dressed and walked to our parish church, The Lady of Mt. Carmel, which was about a mile away. I wanted to thank God for my deliverance at His house. It was still very early, not even six in the morning and some altar boys were preparing the altar for the six o'clock mass. I knelt at one of the pews thanking God in deep prayer. I knew that I was saved from strangulation because my conscience was clear of any wrong doing. Had I been guilty of any misdeed, I knew I wouldn't have the unwavering confidence of God's deliverance and the alien force controlling my hands would have choked me to my death. I would have died from my own hands and my husband who was sleeping next to me would have been blamed for my murder.

The Lady of Mt. Carmel Church at our parish in 1975 was embellished with statues of different saints standing next to the structural columns of the church walls. The pew where I knelt was next to one of these statues and when I looked up after my deep prayer, I saw the eyes of this statue with an evil glow glaring down at me. I was so horrified. I looked at another statue and he was the same, I looked at another and I saw the same thing. All of them had glowing eyes and they were all glaring down at me with an evil look, even that of Jesus, Mary and Joseph. I was stunned horrendously. I hurriedly ran away from the church saying, "Not in your house, not in your house!" I was gravely horrified.

As a catholic in the 70's, it was not a practice to carry the Bible to church. A prayer book or a missal was brought to church instead. As soon as I got back home, I grabbed the Bible. I opened the Bible and when I looked down at the page, I read "God dwells not in temples made by hands." I was amazed, it happened again. The Bible opened once again to the precise page where I could find the answer to the overwhelming question in my mind. At home, I had a small altar with a crucifix and the statuette of the blessed Mary in my bedroom and when I looked at them, they too had evil glowing eyes that were glaring at me. I called on to one of my maids in horror, "Marilyn, come here at once!" As soon as Marilyn appeared, I told her, "Take that crucifix and that statuette out of my room! Throw them to the dumpster, burn them, I don't care what you do with them, I don't want them in my room anymore!" I could no longer hide my condition. It was apparent to Marilyn that something was wrong with me. Any catholic who had witnessed what I did would have definitely concluded that I was possessed by Satan.

While I was an Instructor at MIT, I opened a dress shop and I hired seamstresses to work for me. I had a fashion mannequin at our display window. I chose this particular mannequin because of her angelic face but during those horrible moments, her face too was transformed into a demonic expression with glowing eyes also glaring at me. I kept turning her backward to me so that I wouldn't see her face but for some reason, every time I looked at her, she would be looking back at me tormenting me with a demonic face as if she was turning around all by herself.

When I started to feel the manifestation of this archetype I was terrorized. I started to question my sanity, was I losing my mind? I quickly found out that to doubt your sanity was very bad because it seemed to be progressive. The more you fear that you are going insane the more you go insane, fear of insanity is self-fulfilling. I felt better when I rejected the thought that I was going insane. I felt that my sanity was more stable when I started to believe that evil possession was a real phenomenon. I felt that I could generate more strength to fight mentally by believing that the demonic suggestions that were coming to my mind was not my own but an outside force that was trying to possess me. I was trained from my youth never to entertain evil thoughts and so, with this strong conviction, I started to wage my war against the devil. I reaffirmed myself, "I am a good person who never entertained these kinds of evil thoughts, it could not be me, it is the devil!" I decided that it was healthier for my mind to think that way.

I was completely lost; things were happening that science cannot explain. My only recourse was to ask God for strength to overcome Satan who was bent on overcoming my reasoning to turn me into a murderer. I opened the Bible again and once again it opened to where the words of Jesus said, "You don't need to go to the synagogue to pray, go to your closet and pray in secret". What was I to do? I was completely lost and once again begged God for help. Suddenly, I heard a deep commanding voice which said, "I am the Lord thy God who spoke to Abraham." I have heard of a Biblical character named Abraham but since I had never read the Bible I didn't really know who Abraham was. But to hear an authoritative voice coming from nowhere was overwhelming and I was completely convinced that it was God's voice speaking to me. I was so uplifted and relieved, "I am not worthy but you have come to my aid, thank you so much!" I was assured that God would not let Satan triumph over me.

It did not take long for me to find out that this voice who told me that he was God was a false god. This false god asked me to go to Luneta Park and promised that he would make an apparition, so I hurriedly dressed up, took the bus and went. Then this fake god told me that I had passed the entire test and it was time to anoint me. This fake god asked me to announce to the multitude gathered at the park that I was the anointed queen of hearts. I was torn between humility and obedience when these words came to my mind, "humble yourself before God and he will lift you up." I asked this voice proclaiming to be God, "Please do the announcing so that they would believe." Complete silence followed and after a minute of deafening silence, I knew I had been duped. I angrily cried out to this fake god, "You are not my God, you stay away from me!"

The torture persisted. It was as if I could hear everyone's thoughts; it was as if I had become a telepath. There was no peace in my mind. I knew it was my punishment for delving in the occult and I knew I had to bear it.

Before this entire horrendous ordeal, my husband brought home books of Ruth Montgomery. Ruth Montgomery wrote about spirit guides in the hereafter who are willing to be our guide if we could connect to them through automatic writing. She said that the spirit guide would write messages to us through our own hands controlled by the spirit. She advised that one has to hold a pen over a piece of paper while meditating. She said that to connect with a spirit takes time. She had a friend who tried several times, maybe eight times before a meaningless figure 8 finally was scribbled by her hand which was controlled by the spirit guide. Ruth Montgomery advised that one must have patience.

I was challenged. It was a time in my life when my study of science started to make me a skeptic. Did God create man or did man create God? This is how all these sign of Jonah episode started. I decided to try automatic writing and I said to myself, if it works then it would prove that there is God because God is a spirit. I had a study room in my home. I closed the door to have privacy. I didn't want my maids to see me trying this insanity.

I laid a pad of blank paper on the study desk and adjusted my seat to get myself into a comfortable posture preparing myself for what I expected to be a long wait in one position. I held the pen over the paper making sure that my hand was in a comfortable position. I closed my eyes and started to meditate. I wasn't expecting anything to happen at my first try as what Ruth Montgomery had advised but to my big surprise, I felt a jolt on my chair. Was it my cat? I had a pet but I thought he wasn't in the room with me. Next, I felt some sort of warmth radiating to both my hands and then my right hand started to move and I swear, it was not through my effort that my hand was moving. I was astounded. I kept my eyes closed so I did not know what my hand was doing but it seemed to be scribbling a note on the pad. Fear started to creep within me and my heart started pounding fast. The unknown is indeed terrifying. I concentrated on keeping my heart to beat normally and when my hand stopped scribbling I opened my eyes. Sure enough, my cat was not in the room. What was that jolt I felt on my chair?

It was a creepy short scribble but a friendly greeting, definitely not my handwriting; it was upright and trembly whereas my handwriting is slanted towards the right without any trembling. The note read, "Good morning, I am Good Rose." It was the beginning of my connection to my spirit guide Good Rose. I asked a question and it promptly answered. I did this wild adventure to the occult during a two week semester break. As soon as school opened that October, I told my fellow faculty members that I successfully tried automatic writing. I told them that I ask a question and it answers. One fellow, Jess was his name if I remember right, who worked at the registrar's office was visiting the faculty room and he asked Good Rose how he lost his wrist watch. Good Rose responded. "You went drinking with your friends. You had too much to drink and you passed out. Your friends did not have enough money to pay the bill and they paid it with your watch". Everyone was amazed when Jess confirmed that indeed it was what happened and when he awoke, he was back in his apartment without his wrist watch.

A lady faculty member was impressed and she eagerly asked another question, "Who broke the windshield of my car?" Unhesitatingly, Good Rose scribbled a short answer: "The man who thought you bumped him". The lady faculty member was suddenly wide eyed and she told me in amazement, "I believe you because I don't know you and I never told you what happened". She started telling us the story about a pedestrian who was side swept by the car in front of her while she was driving towards the college campus. The pedestrian went tumbling down the sidewalk and the car that hit him sped away, it was a hit and run. She stopped, intending to help but when the pedestrian got up, he was so enraged thinking that she was the one who bumped him. She got scared and sped away and turned into the college campus and parked. After her classes were over, she found her car with shattered windshield. She told me, I never told you that story and she was completely convinced. I was so amazed myself that I was fortune telling. It was astounding and at the same time scary. Shortly after these fortunetelling episodes, I started to feel the horrifying nefarious energy that was compelling me to become a murderer and I knew I have made a terrible mistake of engaging in the occult.

Jess was so convinced and he brought another gentleman to me who wanted some questions answered by Good Rose but I declined. I told them that I no longer want to engage in automatic writing because it is a very dangerous activity but I did not elaborate on why it was dangerous. Shortly after, I was forced to abandon my post at the University because the compulsion to commit murder had become so formidable.

I must bear the punishment. Satan was relentless. One day, the menacing voice of Satan commanded my heart to stop beating and sure enough my heart beat started to get fainter and fainter. I waged a vigorous mind war against Satan; I concentrated on my heart to beat normally. I fought furiously to my mental exhaustion until I fainted. My husband caught me before I fell on the floor. I was so thankful when I awoke that I was alive but the torture continued. I heard voices from everywhere nonstop for 24 hours day after day after day and sleep deprivation was beginning to take its toll on me. Amidst this cacophony of voices, I heard something referring to Albert Einstein and Sigmund Freud but I could not make out what they were trying to say. I kept asking my youngest sister Elizabeth if Einstein or Freud were still alive and I knew she thought I really had lost my mind.

As a young woman I was a devout Catholic who prayed the rosary every day. I stopped the practice when I became a skeptic but when I was confronted with this force, which was beyond my comprehension, my only recourse was to say the rosary again because that was the only kind of prayer I knew. I had always talked to God when I was still a believer but as a Catholic, I never really considered talking to God as praying because I was taught that to pray was to say the rosary. So, when I was fighting off Satan, I took my old rosary stashed away in my drawer and started saying the rosary again. Every night, I went to bed with the rosary in my hand.

My rosary was made of glass beads linked together by steel chains and a crucifix. One night, I was awakened by something moving. Lo and behold it was my rosary moving by itself. I saw beads, chains, all climbed up the palm of my hand on its own with the crucifix on top. Then an ungodly force took hold of my hand to hold the rosary into a tight grip, so tight that the steel crucifix almost punctured the skin of my fingers and palm of my hand. This ungodly force held my hand so tight my fingers were grotesquely twisted, and it was hurting me. I was bewildered. The weapon that I thought would save me turned into something that was hurting me. I thought I was dreaming but I was not. I was greatly relieved when the force left my hand before the metal cross went through my skin. Deeply puzzled, I put the rosary away and went back to sleep. In the morning, I was curious to see if it was safe to touch the rosary again but as soon as I held it in my hand the same thing happened. When my hand was released from the mysterious forceful grip the rosary fell on the floor and I did not want to pick it up, I did not want to touch it again.

My husband saw the rosary lying on the floor. He picked it up and tried to hand it to me. I refused to take it from him, and I saw that he noticed my uncharacteristic refusal. He persuaded me to take it but there was no way I would touch it again so he said, "It's only a rosary, look I will wear it around my neck." He wore the rosary around his neck and later on he took a nap. When he lay down for his nap the beads of the rosary must have gone under his back. He woke up complaining of a burning pain on the skin of his back. He asked me to see what it could be. I did not see anything out of the normal and I told him so. Later on, he asked me to look at his back again because it was still hurting. When I looked, I saw rounded blisters on his skin. The blisters were the exact imprints of the beads of the rosary. I told him what I saw, I told him that the rosary had burned him, but he would not believe it. When the blisters dried up, the new skin, which was lighter than the older skin, clearly showed the imprint of the rosary. I saw a row of ten little round lighter skin, then a gap, then one little round lighter skin, then another gap followed by ten more little round lighter skin.

I was lost when I realized that I had lost my rosary as a weapon. I desperately pleaded to God, "I don't know how to pray, please teach me how to pray, the rosary is the only prayer I know." Then I heard the sound of my own voice. I heard myself talking to God in my own words and not memorized prayers. I recognized that it was something I had done in the past. As I heard myself talking to God, the memory of exactly what I was doing at that time and where I was, also came to my mind. Then I heard my voice again, also talking with God and I remembered that this next incident had happened on an earlier date. It happened again and again. Someone, somewhere, recorded all my past personal communications to God and they were played back for me to hear. Each incident evoked the memory of where I was and what I was doing at the time. I heard my voice getting younger and younger until I sounded like a little girl who was just beginning to talk talking to God. It was actually a delightful experience to hear my voice as a little girl as it was bewildering. It was as if God was telling me, "You know how to pray. You have been praying to me all your life." What archetype would have caused this if it was not God?

I was seated on a chair at my living room when I started feeling floating in air. I immediately dismounted from my chair before it could carry me up and then the chair would tilt to the side so that I would fall to my death. As soon as I was up on me feet and I looked, I saw the chair landed on the floor. This levitation happened repeatedly during my sign of Jonah ordeal. After a nefarious energy took control of my hands to strangle myself, I knew this evil energy that was manifesting to me was trying to kill me. I did not give it a chance to do me any harm.

Other people around me, just like my maid Marilyn, started noticing that I was not behaving normally and my condition became obvious to everyone especially when I got caught off guard responding to the voices that I was hearing. At that time Elizabeth was a medical student at the University of the Philippines and she was a medical intern at the Philippine General Hospital. My sister Anita, who is three years older that Elizabeth, had become a nurse and she was recruited by an American agent to work in the U.S. a year before. Elizabeth, my mother and my husband brought me against my will to Dr. Ting Leynes, a psychiatrist at PGH whom Elizabeth knew. I was small, weighing only 90 pounds and they had no problem carrying me off my feet to the car in spite of my protestations. "You don't know what force I am fighting against, no one can help me!" I protested. Before Elizabeth decided to take me to the shrink, she told me that I was creating a world of my own. I knew she was deeply concerned for me because tears were rolling down her cheeks. All these proclaimed psychoanalytic experts have not experienced the phenomenon that was manifesting to me so what would they know? They know nothing.

When we got to the hospital, I heard Satan once again maniacally commanding my heart to beat faster, faster. My heart started pounding faster and faster against my chest and again I waged my mind war against Satan, mentally controlling my heart to beat normally. I could imagine what was going on in the minds of my husband, Elizabeth, and my mother who were witnessing my incessant vigorous mumbling as I fought Satan off but I did not care anymore, I must fight. I knew if I failed to make my heart beat normally, its fast beating could lead to cardiac arrest so I fought with all my might and once again I fainted out of exhaustion. I was lying on the couch at the Psychiatrist's office when I awoke.

The Psychiatrist's diagnosis was schizophrenia, some kind of mental condition, but did she mean I was having a mental disorder? That was unacceptable to me. I was fully aware of what was going on. What I was experiencing was real and not a mental disorder. I thought she did not know the force of Satan. I had to make a weekly visit to her and I looked forward to each session with her because she was a very good listener and I needed someone to vent out what I was going through. She gave me some white pills to take. I don't know what those pills were and I can't remember if I took them or not. I think I took one pill and since the voices persisted, I stopped taking the rest. The voices continued to torture me non-stop. That was when I read the Revelation of the Bible aloud. Satan threatened that if he could not take me, he would take my children. I looked at my children and when I saw their innocent mirth I knew Satan could not touch them.

Although I was going through this horrendous ordeal I continued my daily routine of taking my little ones, who at that time were ages 6, 4 and 3, to their bed at night. I couldn't read them stories as I usually did but I stayed with them in their shared room until they had fallen asleep. It was five nights before Christmas. I was still with my little ones after they had gone to sleep when I felt a burning pain on my wrist. I thought I had cut myself but I did not see any cut on my skin. I thought, maybe I touched some hot pepper or some sort of acid? I went to sleep with my wrist hurting but when I awoke in the morning, the pain was gone. The following night, the same thing happened but the pain was on my other hand. I knew it would go away in the morning so I ignored it. The voices that were tormenting me did not allow me to bother about the physical pain I was feeling. The following night, the pain was on one of my foot and then the next night it was on the other foot. I just kept ignoring it because I knew it would be gone in the morning but on the night before Christmas, the pain was on my chest and suddenly, I was jolted into the realization that the pain that I was made to feel ware the wounds of Jesus in his crucifixion. I was stunned. I was made to feel the stigmata without the physical wound. I broke down in tears and prostrated myself on the floor, ever so grateful, thanking Jesus for making me feel his presence. I was assured that he was with me and I knew I would overcome. I just have to be patient.

On New Year 's Eve, I heard a groaning voice of a man which sounded like something very wrong had happened. It was followed by the panicking voice of a young woman calling him, "uncle, uncle!" I recognized the groaning voice was that of my father and the young woman was their maid. My mother and father's home was on the same block where my home was. My home was on one end and theirs was close to the opposite end of the block. I dashed out of my home towards my parent's home running as fast as I could but when I got in front of their place, as I stood on the road, I saw through their wide open living room window, my mother and father in normal conversation, nothing bad had happened at all, they didn't look as happy as they should be on that New Year's eve, rather more concerned and it was probably because of me, and that precipitated the end of my resistance. Satan finally found my breaking point. I cried out to Satan, "Don't do this to me again! If I have to be insane, let me be insane, just don't do this to me again!" Satan found my weakness; I could not take any bad news about my love ones. I gave up the fight, but before my sanity was completely lost, I heard a voice coming from my heart. It was my own voice and with every beat of my heart, a word came out in slow monotone "my mind will stay in its normal condition, my mind will stay in its normal condition" repeatedly going on and on. My mind was stunned back to normalcy. As I listen to my own voice in a monotone chant coming from my heart, I looked up to God in the star laden night sky, "I know it is you, thank you." The voices had gone, there was peace in my mind again. My ordeal was over. With tears running down my cheeks, I slowly walked back home. After three long torturous months, the dragon who swallowed me could not digest me in his belly and he vomited me out back to my freedom so that I could live my normal life once again. I started the New Year of 1976 triumphant over Satan, with full confidence that Satan will never bother me again.

Unbeknownst to me, a task so great will be laid on my shoulders 22 years later. I remember the Bible opening to passages about a strong angel with a little book and while I was reading it, the vision I saw was myself as a teenager with my little book, The Imitation of Christ, which I carried with me everywhere I went, reading it on the bus going to school or whenever I had time to read it. I am sure that this little book was a powerful weapon that enabled me to overcome Satan.

To confirm that I was indeed free from Satan, I went to my kitchen and opened the drawer with knives. I touched the knives and there was joy in my heart. It was such a relief that I did not feel the compelling impulse to grab the knife and stab someone anymore. Thank you, God! I was looking for something at my study room. When I opened the lowest drawer of my desk, the crucifix and the statuette of Mary were there. Marilyn did not discard them. No Catholic would. I held them in my hands. Their kindly holy countenances were back. Satan used them to torment me. I did not want them back in my room. I did not want any religious altar anymore. I left them in the drawer. The angelic face of my mannequin was also back. Everything was back to normal.

My sessions with Dr. Ting Leynes, my psychiatrist, continued until she decided that I didn't need her anymore. It was apparent that I was back to my normal self. On my last session with her, I was surprised when she brought me to a meeting hall full of people who had so many questions to ask me. I remember that there were some Caucasians, but I did not know where they were from. One question I remember I was asked was if I expected to hear voices. My response was, "No, Ruth Montgomery did not say anything about hearing voices." Why were so many people interested in my case? Is it because I snapped out of the schizophrenic state? Is this something uncommon? I never knew the answer.

I heard of well documented episodes of alien hand syndrome many years later, which gave me comfort because to know that I was not the only one to experience such a horrific phenomenon was comforting. On this documentary, all those afflicted with alien hand syndrome were all in terror, not at all like me who confronted this demonic energy fearlessly and I did not develop the syndrome. It happened once and when I overcame it, it never happened again.

Every time I hear news about senseless killings, I am reminded of this horrendous ordeal. I knew the nefarious energy which tried to control my mind to commit senseless killings is the same negative energy that successfully controlled these morally bankrupt individuals who perpetrated senseless hideous murders. I searched for a scientific explanation of what had happened to me while I moved on to raise my three little children. I never really admitted to anyone at that time about the compulsion to kill, not even to Dr. Ting Leynes, because I did not want to be locked up in an asylum in case they deemed me a danger to society, so no one really knew the severity and the horror of what I went through. I don't really know if there is anyone else aside from me who had a temporary bout of schizophrenia which lasted for only three months although those were the longest three months I had ever experienced in my life. I have lived a normal obscure life since then and I am sure that all the people whom I worked with until I retired when I turned 62, including my boss Shane Ames, could attest to the fact that I am a normal sane human being free of any kind of psychosis.

CHAPTER 3

The Collective Unconscious

Years went by so fast. The father of my children abandoned us in 1977 to be with another woman. I did not want the added emotional aggravation demanding child support from him. If he was a responsible father, he would have given his children financial support without me demanding it. Since I did not ask, he did not give any. I raised my children single handedly until they were done with college.

Exactly twenty-two years after my sign of Jonah ordeal, before the year 1997 ended, I had another God experience. I was newly married to Den, my present husband and we were on our honeymoon in Merida, Mexico to see the ancient Mayan temples. We were at the foot of the Mayan temple Uxmal. My mind was filled with images of how the Mayan priest brutally ripped off the beating heart of a human sacrifice and sacrificed it to their god. Suddenly and completely unexpected, Biblical images intruded my thoughts. I saw Abraham with a dagger in his hand raise up to slaughter his son, but an angel came to stop him from committing such a heinous murder. The vision of the god of the children of Israel telling them to kill everything that breathes in the land of their inheritance, immediately followed, and then I saw images reminding me of my own sign of Jonah ordeal. These visions were followed by telepathic message that Satan was behind all these orders to kill human beings. God told me that Satan tried to turn the religion of Abraham into a human sacrificing religion, but He sent the angel to stop him. God told me that Satan took advantage of the belief of the children of Israel that they were the chosen people and successfully urged them to commit genocide. God told me that he will never contradict his law – DO NOT KILL. Satan is behind any false god who tell people to kill.

I could no longer pay attention to our tour guide who was telling us the purpose of the structures we were visiting. I was physically on earth, but my consciousness was with God. I asked God, "Why are you talking to a sinner like me?" That was when I was shown a complete vision of my entire life and then God walked me through the Commandments one by one.

As soon as we were back in Florida, I felt the unstoppable urge to open the Bible. At that time, all my children had come back home after college. I was the one who moved to Den's apartment when I married him taking only my suitcase of clothing. I left my Bible at my home with my children. I asked Den if he has a Bible, and I was glad when he found one stashed in his bookshelves. I did not want to cause any rift in my new marriage. Den was a professor of science subjects. While Den was watching TV at the living room, I went to the balcony to read the Bible. Since I was raised a Catholic when the clergy did not encourage Bible reading without clergy supervision to avoid interpretations contrary to theirs, I did not know what to look for and where to find them. Lo and behold, as soon as I sat on the balcony chair and laid the Bible on the table, the Bible opened by itself, the text that God wanted me to read floated out of the page and were magnified a hundredfold followed by images of what they mean just as what happened during my sign of Jonah ordeal. I was astounded, I was witnessing a miracle once again.

During a commercial break of the TV program Den was watching, I asked him, "What would you say if I tell you that some truths were revealed to me? It has something to do with collective beliefs." His response was, "Dr. Carl Gustav Jung has a theory of the collective unconscious." I have heard of Dr. Jung, but I didn't know about his works. I went to the bookstore and looked for books of Dr. Jung. Many were too highly technical for me to understand. I am an Architect and psychoanalysis is nowhere in my field of studies. I was very glad when I found the book - Jung for Beginners by Jon Platania. I easily understood what Dr. Jung was saying because I am a witness of the manifestations of archetypes emanating from our collective unconscious. I know it is hard to believe something you did not experience but it is a blessing that you did not encounter what I encountered because if you did not have the ability to face this encounter fearlessly, you will be traumatized to the point of loosing your sanity.

It was not easy to express what I experience fighting off the devil possession attempt of Satan but with Dr. Jung's perception of this paranormal force, I found the terminology to express what happened to me. Dr. Jung's perception of the collective unconscious was vindication for me, that I did not have a brain disorder. What Dr. Jung called the negative dynamic archetype, created by thoughts in the collective that are evil, destructive, perverse and superstitious, manifested to me. Its opposite archetype, the positive dynamic archetype, created by kind, loving, good, benevolent and generous thoughts was the one that possessed Mother Theresa that drove her to do her admirable deed helping the poor.

As I am looking back to my horrendous sign of Jonah ordeal, considering Dr. Jung's perception of the collective unconscious, I now believe that those who are diagnosed as having schizophrenia are actually people whose brain frequency are attuned to that of the collective unconscious and they are experiencing another person's thought process. A schizophrenic may say that there is a clock on the wall when there is physically no clock on the wall where she is, but what is happening is that her brain is receiving the thought of another person who is looking at a clock on the wall. From my own experience, I would say that to be attuned to the collective unconscious can truly damage the brain of one who is not ready for it. First of all, at the initial shock of this experience, one can be engulfed with tremendous fear, because the unknown is truly terrifying and the phobia alone will cause severe psychosis. If I did not have a perfectly clear conscience from any wrong doing, I would probably had gone insane because I would not have the weapon to fight against it. What saved me was my firm conviction that God will never forsake me because I am a good person and this was how I overcame the overwhelming fear that engulfed me at the start.

While I was in this state that Dr. Ting Leynes, the psychiatrist, called schizophrenia, I heard a voice saying, "You marvel at your technological inventions of the telephone, what do you think of what you are able to do right now?" I did not understand at that time what it meant. Now that I am looking back, did that voice mean my ability to hear other people's thoughts? Hearing other's thoughts all at the same time was sheer torture. There was so much noise in my mind but I knew I had to bear it with the hope that it would somehow end and all I had to do was to be patient for as long as I can. If I lose my patience, I knew I would completely lose my sanity. I was hearing horrible thoughts that I could not believe a person whom I knew was capable of thinking. I did not want to hear it. Are we destined to become telepaths as we evolve? There will be no more falsifying of anything when that happens and corruptions of any kind will be non-existent. Humanity would no longer have a need for Julian Assanges or Edward Snowdens. But today we are definitely not ready for this ability based on what I experienced. Perhaps when we humans are more pure in mind, it would not be as torturous as what I had experienced.

During my sign of Jonah ordeal, I was puzzled by the vision I saw of some sort of energy radiating from the head of all humans and gathering as one, suddenly, I realized what it meant. Our thoughts are energies that do not dissipate into nothing but are radiated out of the confines of our skull to become our collective unconscious where archetypes are created by collective beliefs that can manifest at random to interfere with our activities. We all get connected to the collective unconscious when we are dreaming, and we get disconnected when we awake. There are some who for reasons still unknown, do not get disconnected when they wake up and they react to both the archetypes they encounter from the collective unconscious and to reality, they are diagnosed as afflicted by schizophrenia. Is this an evolutionary process? We are told that we are only utilizing 10% of our brains. What happens when we utilize the whole 100% capacity of our brains, are we going to be able to communicate telepathically, by mental telepathy? I believe that dreams are irrefutable evidence of the existence of our collective unconscious.

Hundreds of apparitions of Mary or the lady in white are reported to the Vatican resulting from the idolatrous worship of the image of Mary and the repeated prayers of the rosary and litanies defying the edict that forbids images and what Jesus said, do not say repeated prayers. Worshipping Jesus as god created the apparitions that created religions like the Shakers and the Mormons, which cannot give up the patriarchal role of man, and woman are subjugated, the same as Islam. God sent me, a woman, to attest to the fact, that man and woman are equal.

Stigmata is the direct result of worshipping the crucified image of Jesus. I saw a program on TV that delved into this subject of stigmata. I saw how wounds burst out of the skin of a woman, on her forehead, hands, feet, mimicking the wounds of Jesus, demonstrating the violent energy that results from worshipping the crucified image of Jesus. St. Francis was an avid worshipper of the crucifix, and he had stigmata. This is one of the reasons that this Commandment forbids worshipping any image, the collective energies of the act of worshipping the deities would create the apparition, which enhances the superstition and prevents attainment of intellectual purity that is necessary to evolve into a higher level of existence.

Both Judaism and Christianity believe that God was just testing the faith of Abraham when he was asked to kill his son as sacrifice. These collective false beliefs resulted in Mohammad creating a religion that worships this false god that require human sacrifice that are now a big problem of humanity. Muslims are convinced they are ordained by their false god to kill non-Muslims. I have very good friends who are Muslims, but they do not want to discuss religion. I pray that they realize that even if they do not participate in the act of killing, their proclamation that Muhammad is a prophet of god embolden those who carry out his violent words to kill infidels to their false faith and all of them are therefore guilty of the killing and are in danger of being cast to the lake of fire. In fact all Abrahamic religions who refuse to believe me that the god who told Abraham to kill his son as sacrifice was the negative dynamic archetypal god who is none other than Satan are also emboldening the terrorists who are worshipping this false god at the Kaaba on their annual Haj festival in Mecca, therefore they too are not guiltless in the death of innocent victims of Islamic terrorism.

During the time of Joan of Arc, the French believed in the legend of the maid of Lorraine who would come to save them, then an archetype created by these collective beliefs and legend manifested to Joan of Arc that possessed her to do her heroic deeds. She was burned on the stake for heresy and later canonized by the church as a saint.

There is a movie – A Beautiful Mind – about Dr. Nash who experienced the manifestation of an archetype that emanated from the collective unconscious created by the collective American paranoia towards Communism. Dr, Nash was successful in perceiving the archetypes from the collective unconscious and separating them from what was reality and he managed to live a meaningful life despite his obvious bout with schizophrenia.

I emailed the Science Channel about my views on the Paranormal Caught on Camera program on TV but I was repeatedly ignored. I told them that their show is perpetuating superstitions. Collective belief in ghosts added to preexisting legends create the archetype that visually manifests as ghosts. The Science Channel proudly claims that more paranormal are caught on camera. Of course, their show is captivating the attention of those who take pleasure on ghosts stories, that boosts the archetype that manifests as ghosts. It is a money-making undertaking for them so they would rather perpetuate the superstitions rather than expose the truth that will lead mankind to attaining purity of mind to reach perfection required to achieve the perfection of Jesus. Ghosts are not souls of the dead, which are either reincarnated or cast to the lake of fire. I saw their TV videos of how these ghostly manifestations can pull the legs of a sleeping man up until only his shoulders were touching the bed when the man was awakened. I too had a levitation experience. I saw images of the soldiers at war during the civil war caught on TV. The Civil war stories are still fresh in the minds of Americans, which they relive annually, no wonder they make visual manifestations that emanated from the collective unconscious.

Many are becoming unbelievers of God. Scientists observed some energy that is beyond their comprehension, so they call it dark energy. Dark because they are in darkness as to what it really is, but they know it comprises much more than half of our universe. I saw that as intelligent beings from all over our universe reach perfection to metamorphose into pure energy, so does our universe expands. I am not a scientist, all I can say is what the SPA showed me, Whether the pure energy that resulted from the purification of an intelligent being becomes what science call dark energy, I have no way of knowing but I know it is sentient energy because it evolved from intelligent beings. I am positive that a high source of knowledge communicated with me. It is not easy to believe what you have not experienced but I had a God experience, or maybe I tapped into some higher source of knowledge that communicated with me through visions and mental telepathy. It showed me that it had communicated to us intelligent beings from the dawn of civilization and our ancestors with limited knowledge of their surroundings interpreted the messages that they received according to their level of understanding of our world. It showed me that we, intelligent beings, are the larvae of God and that is the purpose of life. It showed me that the body of Jesus disappeared because together with his consciousness or what we call soul, it metamorphosed into pure energy to become one with God which can only happen when one reaches that level of perfection to warrant the process of metamorphosis.

The Commandments that Moses received from God is the laws of life. Violate these laws and the soul or consciousness will eventually terminate, no more life, no more thinking, dead forever and the residual energy becomes what appeared to me as the Higgs-Boson particle responsible for the cohesion of elements to become physical matter, and in the vision given to me, this occurs in the magma mantle of earth, thus, the ancients who were given the vision called it the lake of fire. Our choice is whether we violate the Commandments or the laws of life to become the dirt of the earth since magma cools down to become rock that erodes to become dust or follow the Commandments until we reach that level of perfection to metamorphose into pure energy to become one with God. The choice is ours. Follow the false prophet who is leading his followers to commit the most grievous offence, to kill another human, and the termination of your consciousness is assured. Now it is clear why Jesus said, forgive, love your enemy, because by doing so, you are prevented from killing.

Although I have journeyed into the bizarre and perilous world of schizophrenia, I swear that I never lost control of my mind. My ordeal lasted only for three months but it was the longest and the most terrifying three months of my life. I experienced all the bizarre forces and anomalies that confront a schizophrenic. I must admit it took all my inner strength, everything I've got to hold on to my dear life and to my sanity until it was all over. I had to fight with all my might to overcome all the formidable forces that were compelling me to commit hideous abominable deeds. I am aware that my ordeal had caused tremendous strain on the people who loved me as well. I saw them in tears looking at me in my condition. They must have thought, as they watched me react to the forces that were manifesting to me which they could neither hear nor feel, that they had lost me forever to the world of the insane. It was a most terrifying experience that I never wanted to think about ever again. In time however, I gradually learned to deal with this horrible memory. I believe that humanity needs to be enlightened of this fact, we must purge our collective unconscious of all negative thoughts to eradicate the negative dynamic archetype permanently.

Tales of atrocities committed by schizophrenics always stir up my memory of this horrible encounter and it always made me wonder if there is any way I could be of help to alleviate this malady. There are many schizophrenics who are violent because they are easy outlets of the negative dynamic archetype from the collective unconscious. It is because of their inherent violent personality even before they got attuned to the collective unconscious. Perhaps if I share my experience with others, they may understand better what schizophrenia is. Perhaps there are others like me who managed to get out of a schizophrenic state completely unscathed, but I know not one nor have heard of anyone other than myself. There is no permanent cure for this condition, how did I get out of it without medication? Did I hold on to my sanity long enough that my brain switched back to normal? Did the people who loved me pray hard enough that their prayers were answered?

Science cannot explain what causes schizophrenia. I believe I have found an answer. As a firsthand witness to this phenomenon, I believe I can explain what causes schizophrenia. Schizophrenia is a state where one's consciousness is attuned to the collective unconscious simultaneous with reality. To tell people who are feeling these kinds of manifestations that they are only imagining it, is doing them more harm. To tell them that these are things that they are creating in their minds is more devastating because you are reinforcing their fear of insanity. I felt so frustrated that nobody believed I was fighting against an unseen force. I was alone in my war against the devil, and you better believe that it did not feel good. I am sure I would have felt better if someone had shown me sympathy by believing in me rather than insisting to me that I was imagining it. I was furious when I was told that I was a schizophrenic who was creating my own world. It was so frustrating to be with people who thought that they knew better than what I perceived was happening.

Science explains that schizophrenia is a condition caused by chemical imbalance in the brain. They say that schizophrenics create a world of their own, they say that the experience is confined only within the imagination of the afflicted. I vehemently disagree. I did not create nor imagine the forces that confronted me when I was in that chaotic state called schizophrenia. I was not delusional nor was I hallucinating. The forces that I encountered were very real forces which were not my own. Dr. Carl Gustav Jung perceived the phenomenon of the collective unconscious and the archetypes that come from the collective unconscious that carry specific energy that can act upon the world. However, many dismiss him as a mystic because his discovery is beyond human comprehension. I believe that the profoundness of his discovery had been proven over and over through the ages through the various unexplainable experiences of mankind. The problem is that the experts in the field of psychology and psychiatry cannot associate these unexplainable phenomena with the perception of Dr. Jung.

I believe that a schizophrenic is a person whose brain has somehow undergone a kind of mutation and has become permanently attuned to the collective unconscious. I was lucky I got disconnected from the collective unconscious before my endurance wore off, otherwise, I would have been mentally impaired since then, and by now I will not be in the position of explaining my ordeal. No human is prepared for this condition because the state of our collective unconscious is in complete disarray, chaotic, violent, full of hate and perversions, disorganized and destructive. I believe that this is due to the fact that mankind in general has not acknowledged the existence of the collective unconscious. Mankind is not aware of the archetypes he is creating that are affecting humanity. It is for this reason that I would like to share with you this knowledge that I have acquired about this phenomenon. I believe there is no human who can hold on to his or her sanity once permanently attuned to the collective unconscious, except those who have the soundness of mind and purity of conscience like me. Science tries to alleviate the bizarre experiences of the afflicted by some kind of medications to put the chemicals in their brain in "equilibrium" but the medication is temporary and has to be taken for the rest of their lives. If the medication is stopped the afflicted goes right back to the chaotic state of schizophrenia. Science has not found the permanent cure for this condition and perhaps they never will. Could it be possible that the mutation that happens to the afflicted is the next step of human evolution, but we are trying very hard to avoid it? I believe that for now the only way we can help schizophrenics is to organize our collective unconscious and purge it of destructive evil thoughts.

During my sign of Jonah ordeal, I encountered forces of different archetypes our collective unconscious creates. In the seventies, the minds of millions were geared into the subjects of evil possession, exorcism and poltergeist. The movie theaters and television stations were saturated with this topic. These millions of collective thoughts generated an energy, which everyone was not aware of. Everyone was doing it unconsciously. This is what Dr. Jung calls the collective unconscious. The collective thoughts on evil possession generated an archetype. Dr. Jung said this archetype possesses its own specific energy and is capable of manifesting and this was the first archetype that I encountered. I experienced a force that was trying to overcome my reasoning to control my being to commit evil things. My reasoning could not explain this phenomenon and that was what made the experience so terrifying. I did not know about the phenomenon of the collective unconscious at that time. The unknown is always quite terrifying.

Now that I am aware of the phenomenon of the collective unconscious, I tried to identify every archetype that I had encountered but there were some manifestations that I could not attribute to any collective thoughts or beliefs. When I encountered the evil possessor archetype, the only way I knew to counteract it was to go back to God and begged for mercy and help.

The bizarre phenomenon of my rosary moving by itself, what kind of archetype could possibly do that? Archetypes are created by collective beliefs but my rosary moving by itself could not have possibly been caused by an archetype. I know that it is possible that the beads had irritated my husband's skin and had caused the blisters, although many others had slept with beads around their necks and had not gotten blistered. However, the rosary moving by itself is something I could not explain. In the Philippines, the collective belief is that the rosary is a weapon against evil and yet the force that came to me was implying that the rosary was doing me more harm than good. What unseen force can move a physical object? I swear, I witnessed a telekinesis phenomenon, which is not attributable from any archetype. I know that this is a believe-it-or not story but I have no reason to make this up and I definitely did not imagine this nor was I delusional. It really happened. I am sharing it with you because I am looking for an answer. The only valid answer acceptable to me is that it was God telling me that repeated prayers will prevent us from attaining purity of mind to reach perfection. This is why Jesus said, do not say repeated prayers.

And so, everybody thought that I was possessed by the devil. I did not want to touch the rosary and I wanted the religious images to be burned. To the Catholics, these were sacred items, the very tools used in exorcism, which I was rejecting and which I wanted to destroy. To a Catholic's mind I was doing severe sacrilege. I heard later on that one of my relatives went to the Catholic Priest and requested him to perform an exorcism rite for me, but he declined. In the Philippines, Catholicism is the predominant religion. I would expect that the archetype that would prevail from their collective beliefs would be in favor of the propagation of religious images and the rosary. Where did the archetype, which apparently was showing me that these articles of worship were not good for me, come from? I know It was God's way of showing me that I was practicing ways of worship violating His Commandments that will prevent me from attaining purity of mind required to reach perfection.

What archetype among all the entities that I had encountered in my voyage to the schizophrenic world, would fit the end part of my ordeal? Of course, I would like to take it as Divine intervention. I am sure that the prayers of the ones who loved me helped a lot. I absolutely believe in the power of prayers; it works in the same context. Hearing a million voices was being tuned directly to the collective unconscious and not to any archetype. Had I known Dr. Jung's theory about the collective unconscious when I journeyed into the world of schizophrenia, I would probably react differently when the archetypes started to manifest to me. My reasoning would have probably rationalized what was going on and the experience would probably not be as terrifying. However, it was twenty-two years later that I became enlightened of the subject of the collective unconscious after I experienced another believe-it-or not episode in my life which I wrote in a book entitled The Book of Life that was published by Vantage Press Inc. of New York. This encounter was the one that led me to Dr. Jung's theory.

I came to the United States in 1980. In 1994 my dearest father passed away because of a stroke. Four years later, my mother came to visit me in Florida. Every morning during her visit, we had breakfast together and talked about life in the Philippines. One morning, with teary eyes, she expressed her regrets that my father expired while she was out food shopping. She told me about the circumstance around my father's death and it stirred the memory of the last hour of my sign of Jonah ordeal. During that time, I had wondered why I heard the helper's voice and not her voice with the moaning sound of my father. My mother's recount of the incident fit perfectly with what I had heard thirty-one years before. I did not say anything about it to my mother, but I wondered, could I have heard my father's last breath nineteen years before it happened? That was not collective beliefs therefore it couldn't have emanated from the collective unconscious. I believe my consciousness tapped into the future. Was this God's plan so that I would give up the fight to end my ordeal?

That was the last visit of my dearest mother with me in Florida where she stayed for a month. That was when I asked my mother what time of the day I was born because Jesus already made me aware of the recurring second number in my life. She told me, "It was an hour after midnight." I was born on the second hour. It could even be the second minute of the second hour.

If you think that by nurturing hatred in your mind, by nurturing thoughts of hurting someone or killing someone in your mind, you are doing no harm because physically you did not really do it, I am telling you, you are very wrong. A thousand or so of you nurturing the same thoughts will create in the collective a force that will seek to become reality through people who have lost control of their minds or through people of low morality. I have felt this evil force that was seeking to manifest through me during my sign of Jonah ordeal. This evil force is one of the forces that Dr. Jung is talking about which our collective unconscious is creating. This is the force that drives schizophrenics to violence and often times the victims are their loved ones. This is the force that has caused numerous senseless murders, a force so formidable that morally weak mortals cannot control. If you were among those who entertained these destructive evil thoughts, the blood of the victims of these senseless murders is also in your hands even if you were a hundred miles away from the scene of the crime. You have contributed to the force in the collective that sought to become reality in the being of the weak who became the outlet of the energy of the archetype created by your collective thoughts. This is the force that drove Andrea Yates to murder her five little children. We call this force Satan. Satan will be alive and well for as long as there are mortals who dwell on destructive, evil thoughts. If we so desire to get rid of Satan, we all must learn to think of nothing but good. To further purge our collective unconscious, we also must get rid of all superstitious and false beliefs. The choice is ours.

If you think that nurturing perverse thought of sexually assaulting someone in your mind, be it a man, a woman or a child, is not bad because you did it only in your mind, you are very wrong. In the collective these perverse thoughts will seek to manifest in the person of a sexual pervert, and the crime will be perpetrated. This is why in Matthew 5; 27-28, Jesus said: Whosoever, then, looketh on a woman to lust after her, that is, so looks on her as to lust, and cast about to obtain, he is rightly said to commit adultery within his heart. Look at the staggering number of sexual crimes that are being committed in our world. Pornography is protected by the law of the freedom of speech. Can you imagine the magnitude of the force created by collective perverse thoughts triggered by pornography? If you think that pornographic materials are harmless, think again. If you are among those perverts who dwell on these perverse thoughts, the burden of guilt committed by the perverts that has been the outlet of the perverse collective force is also on your shoulders even if you did not partake in the physical act. The perverts who claim that the evil spirit compelled them to commit the crime are telling the truth. I do not condone these weak mortals who have become the outlet of evil forces. If I managed to defy the evil forces that tried to manifest through me, there is no excuse for anyone not to be able to do the same. It is everyone's responsibility to humanity to maintain a strong moral integrity to avoid being the outlet of these atrocious forces.

We do not need to ban pornography and violate the law of freedom of speech. If there is no demand for pornography, publishing it will not be a viable money-making business. This is the law of supply and demand. We were taught from when we were young, not to entertain evil thoughts but we were not given the reason for it, this is why we should never entertain evil thoughts, we boost the energy of the negative dynamic archetype that possess people of low morals and mentally handicapped to commit the crime.

Timothy McVey became the outlet of all militants that have anti-government sentiments. All of them have the blood of the innocent victims of the Oklahoma bombing on their hands. You can see the magnitude of the collective force their hatred has unleashed in the person of Timothy McVey. Are books such as The Turner's Diary harmless? What is its effect on the collective unconscious? Harry Potter books are very popular among children right now. I have not read one, but I heard they deal with some kind of sorcery. What kind of grownups will emerge from the Harry Potter influence. Will these Harry Potter tales affect the collective unconscious adversely? Our beliefs, fears and fantasies also create archetypes in our collective unconscious that will seek to become reality.

If one would go trekking up the Himalayas to go to Mount Everest one has to pray to the god of the mountains for safe passage. You better do so because the spirit of this god is still very strong because of the collective beliefs of the Tibetans. There are so many gods in our world that we create according to our beliefs. The Old Testament of the Bible, the Torah and the Koran all has the same root. In the Middle East, both the Jews and the Moslem pray to the god of their ancestors, the god who led them to war. To this day, there is no peace in their lands. They believe in holy wars. Are they going to wage these holy wars until they all perish? They are both descendants of one father, Abraham. They are brothers. Why can't they hug each other in peaceful settlements to end all this bloodshed for the sake of their future generation? Why don't they confront their god and ask him when would they be led to peace? Their god is an unforgiving god who demands an eye for an eye, a tooth for a tooth. Their god is a god of war, how would this god lead them to peace, he would not know how. They both have a big decision to make. Are they going to pass down to their children and the children of their children the legacy of hatred, war, and suffering which their forefathers handed down to them, or would they choose to be written down in history books as the generation that awoke to the truth and has brought peace to their lands?

When Orson Welles made an announcement on the radio of a Martian landing on our planet Earth to promote a show, he did it in a way that sounded so real it created a mass paranoia, the fear of aliens invading our planet. Then the Roswell incident happened. Since then, men have repeatedly reported seeing the apparition of unidentified flying objects in the sky, then there were reports of alien encounters followed by reports of alien abductions. Ever since the television show entitled X Files came on the television screens, reports of alien abductions quadrupled. I do sympathize with people who had an alien abduction experience, but I believe that they experienced a force that was created by the collective fear of aliens. To them the experience was very real as much as the evil forces that I had experienced were very real, but I do believe that they were both created by the archetypes from our collective unconscious. Believe me, we did not create this in our minds. We got attuned to the collective unconscious.

I have written a book about all my strange experiences because I would like everyone to become aware of the phenomenon of the collective unconscious. When I heard about the student killings at the Columbine School, I sent my manuscript to all the major television networks, to Newsweek and Time magazine publications and to my local newspaper but my story had been ignored. I had my manuscript published at my own expense and entitled it The Book of Life, hoping that I could share my experience with you all through the book because I really believe that the only way we can reach a peaceful existence on our planet Earth is to become aware of the effects of the collective unconscious in our lives. I had sent my book to my congressman and to a very important person to no avail. This is another one of my many attempts to share with you my experience, I hope that this time it will work.

CHAPTER 4

The Appraiser

It was the 5th of January 1976, the fifth day after I overcame my sign of Jonah ordeal. My children and I were at my parent's home where we hang out almost daily. I was seated on my father's favorite rocking chair, wide eyed, pondering over a most harrowing ordeal I had overcome, which started in October and ended just before the new year, just five days ago. The sudden flash of a camera startled me. Mama, my dearest mother, had taken a snapshot photo of me, and my pondering suddenly shifted to what could possibly be the reason why Mama had taken my photograph. This is why that date got stuck indelibly in my mind; I started to ask myself, what was so special about the 5th of January that Mama took my photograph? I could not think of any special event for that date, so I dismissed the thought and decided that she probably had one more shot in the roll of film in her camera that she wanted developed, so she finished it by taking a snapshot of me. My thoughts went back to its previous preoccupation. Why did it happen? Why me? Mama did not want me to talk about it to anyone. She caught me one time answering questions of Myrna, my cousin who was so curious to know about my ordeal, but Mama was so quick to cut short my cousin's inquiry.

Mama wanted me to keep the whole thing hush-hush, which I thought was impossible because there were so many questions in my mind that I needed answered. She wanted me to stop thinking about it for my own good, but the mysterious experience was still very fresh in my mind, and I could not focus on anything else. It was so strange that although I was very relived that I got out of the ordeal alive and sane, I could not stop hoping that the mysterious experience would continue and not stop altogether until I could discover what had caused it and why it had happened. My paranormal encounter started with deception that progressed into being horrific, but it ended in comforting friendship. I knew I should really stop thinking about it and get on with my life. Maybe I could take my mind off of it by putting more effort concentrating on looking for another job. Before my horrifying ordeal, I was a college instructor at the Mapua Institute of Technology. I was a member of the faculty of the MIT School of Architecture and Planning. I felt bad that my ordeal had caused me to end my teaching profession in such an abrupt manner without proper notice, I went AWOL but what had happened was beyond my control and there was no way I could explain it to be understood by the Dean of our school.

My pondering was interrupted once again because the telephone rang. Mama picked up the phone and then announced that Mamang, my mother-in-law was waiting for me at my home to discuss some important matters. My home was on the same block where my parents' home was but on the other end just a few minutes walk away, so I gathered my three little ones and we all started marching back home to see Mamang.

Soledad, my business minded mother-in-law bought real estate properties. I called her Mamang because that was how Egberto Junior, nicknamed Junn, the father of my children, called her. She wanted to build apartments and houses on the lots she bought. One of the Lots was for Junn. She asked me to design a house under Junn's name, but she told me that my husband and I were owners by name only. The Real Estate Department of the Philippine Social Security System granted us a loan to finance the construction of this house, but the Real

Estate Department had requirements that we needed to comply with to release our loan. She wanted me to go to the SSS office to find out what the problem was. I was very glad to get my mind back to my profession. Perfect timing, I thought, it was exactly what I needed, and it was the best therapy to get my mind operating in normal parameters once again. I immediately set my mind in full gear to tackle the task at hand. Designing homes is something I truly enjoy so I was very enthusiastic about trouble shooting the design problem of the project. Mamang also asked me to design a four-unit apartment on another lot that she owned. I did not care what Mamang's motives were. I never got paid for my professional services because Filipino custom dictates that relatives are expected to give out their professional services to their relatives for nothing. Well, I considered the lot where I designed a home for Junn and me and our three children as my fee, which Mamang purchased even if she said it's ours by name only, all the legal documents stated that it was ours. I designed and prepared the construction documents for a four-unit apartment and as soon as I got all the documents ready, I submitted them to the Building Department of Quezon City to acquire a building permit.

The Social Security System of the Philippines was on its early stage of operation where contributions were getting accumulated and claims for benefits were still very few and so they created the Real Estate Department (RED), and it granted home financing exclusively to all the SSS contributors. Since contribution to the SSS is mandatory when one is privately employed, everyone privately employed was a member of the SSS. Government employees were members of the GSIS, or the Government Security Insurance System and they were not qualified to avail themselves of SSS benefits. The interest rate was only 3% for the first P30,000 which was very much lower than what banks demanded so all members of the SSS wanted to avail themselves of their housing loans.

I went to the SSS office to comply with their requirements so that the funds for the construction of our house would be released. It was my first time visiting the twelve-story SSS Building complex because the loan application and all previous transactions were done by Mamang. At the lobby information desk, I was told, "RED is on the fifth floor". There were many other applicants already at the RED waiting room when I got there. I got a number for my turn and sat down on one of the seats. I did not expect that I would need a jacket because Philippine weather was always warm, so I was freezing while waiting for my number to be called at the SSS RED waiting room where the air-conditioner was set at what felt like refrigerator settings. All SSS employees wore an ID tag on their chest, so you know their names right away. Teofilo, a very charming fellow whom everyone called Filo, was the gentleman who called in the applicants. He went through all the documents of new applicants to check if they had complied with all the requirements to process the loan and then he logged in the application on his logbook and gave it a loan processing number if the application papers were found in order. There were two other loan examiners that an applicant had to go through. One loan examiner went through the credit documents and the other was an Appraiser who went through the Architectural plans and construction documents of the house proposed to be built.

Junn and I were the loan applicants and I, at the same time was the project Architect. Edna, a very nice lady Architect whose sweet smile displayed her pretty dimples, was the SSS Appraiser on front desk duty for the week who attended to me. She discovered that I was the Owner- Architect after reviewing my documents. She informed me that the Appraisal division needed more Architects or Engineers for Building Appraisal positions. What a perfect timing once again. To be a building appraiser had never really crossed my mind, but I was ready for a new job. I did not have any idea how it would be to be an appraiser, but I was willing to give it a try. If it turned out that it was not for me, I could always quit and look for another job. To be in Architectural practice on your own, you must develop your clientele. I was not a social butterfly to easily develop a wide group of clienteles and I was new in the field of professional practice. I designed the home of my brother and a cousin, a few clients, and these projects for Mamang and I was a builder too, I have built a couple of houses. I had in mind being a building contractor as a good possibility.

As soon as my documents were accepted for the loan application, I proceeded to the SSS Personnel Department to apply for the job. After my credentials were evaluated, I was called in for physical examination. I found out that the Philippine Social Security System had its own Medical Department on the ground floor of the building complex complete with infirmary and Dental Clinic. I also found out that although the system did not provide medical insurance, all employees were provided free Medical and Dental service right there at their building complex. The job I was applying for was becoming more attractive. Also, the main office was a five-minute drive from home, which was very convenient. However, there was something in the questionnaire about my medical history that caused me some worry. The questionnaire asked if I had any mental disorder of any kind in the past. The ordeal I had just come out of about six weeks ago, was it a mental disorder? My psychiatrist thinks so but no! I could not admit that it was. While I was going through the whole ordeal, I knew I was in full control of my mind. I knew exactly what was going on with every minute that elapsed for the whole three months duration of the ordeal. The proclaimed experts who diagnosed my condition did not know what truly happened to me; in fact, science cannot provide any explanation for the phenomenon I had experienced. I answered the question – No! I did not have any mental disorder. Apparently, the System had no access to my medical history. Two weeks after I filed my application for the job, my employment with the Real Estate Department of the Philippine Social Security System became official on the first of March 1976.

Manang Fely was the first lady I had to report to as a newcomer to RED. She was the RED Personnel manager in charge of attendance, and she saw to it that everyone wore the prescribed uniform to work. She gave me free of charge several yards of double-knit navy-blue polyester fabric good for three dresses, but she told me that I had to pay a dressmaker to sew my uniforms. That was no problem for me because

I sew my own clothes. Being an inch shorter than five feet in height, I managed to make four dresses out of the fabric she gave me, following strictly her instruction to conform to the exact design of the uniform with the skirt not shorter than knee length. After Manang Fely briefed me on all the office rules and regulations, she introduced me to the RED Manager, Mr. Pineda and then brought me to the Appraisal Division and introduced me to my new boss, Attorney Baybay, the Chief of the Appraisal Division. Atty. Baybay had two assistants. Everyone called his assistants Gogoy and Gaving and their clerk Dione oversaw the collection of all the different case folders that needed appraisals or inspections from the Records Section and dispersing them to us appraisers. I was assigned to join Gaving's section.

As a newcomer, I needed to be trained to do my duties. Gaving assigned Fe, one of the lady Appraisers in his Section to be my trainer. I had to follow Fe wherever she went for a couple of weeks and observed how she conducted her building inspections and appraisals. Fe pounded on my head over and over how strict she was and how incorruptible she was and warned me against builders on the site who would try bribery for favorable reports. I was very proud to work with someone who had the dignity to overcome the temptations the job entails who would refuse to accept goodwill gifts usually in cash money that were voluntarily offered to appraisers. It became apparent why the RED employed only certified Architects and Engineers for the Appraisal position. Their professional certification can be revoked for corruption or negligence or incompetence or if they break rules. Getting certified is no easy task; one must go through college and must pass the state board to get it. Why would anyone take the risk that would put their hard-earned professional license in jeopardy?

The camaraderie in the Real Estate Department of the Philippine Social Security System was exemplary. I immediately became part of a big family. Everyone was very pleasant and nice to work with. Everyone was like a brother and a sister or an aunt or an uncle. Aside from Edna, whom I met while she was on counter duty when I applied for my housing loan, and Fe, who was my trainer, I also met Yvonne and I was very enthusiastic to join all of them. Edna and I became very good friends because she was also a mother of three little children the same age as mine. Fe was single so her interests were different. Yvonne, also a mother of a little girl, was a good friend too but she left when her family moved to a different region in the country about a year after I got my employment with the SSS. Other lady appraisers came after me; there was Helen, Eloise, and Lily. Architecture and Building Construction are male dominated professions so in our office there were more male Building Appraisers than female, but we all worked in complete harmony with each other.

I found the working operation of the RED very impressive. The filing system was excellent considering that the RED system was not yet computerized at that time. At any time, a loan applicant can find out what is the status of his or her loan application and who was the personnel currently processing the loan documents or application for loan releases. At the RED Records division, loan status can be traced by its processing number, or applicant's name or address or even just by the date the application was filed. What I saw made me think that the system operated in a way that corruption was non-existent because everyone who processed loan documents was answerable to the cause of the delay of the processing and anyone who was assigned a case must produce a status report within a week after being assigned the case. I was very proud to work in an establishment that I thought was free of corruption.

The SSS operation was far better than what I observed at the Quezon City Building Department when I went to get the building permit for the proposed apartment building of my mother-in-law. Two weeks after I submitted my plans for a building permit, I went back to the Building Department to inquire about the status of the application. I was told to see this man who was so unfriendly and uncooperative who made me feel that I was an annoyance to him. He told me that I needed more details to get my plans examined but he could not tell me what ordinance or code I needed to comply with. All he said was that I should know since I was the Architect. It was so frustrating because to my knowledge I had complied with all the code requirements. As a taxpayer, I expected that this government employee would assist me, to explain to me what part of the code I failed to comply with, if I had misinterpreted it. But this cold uncooperative building department official would not spend any more time with me. He handed me back all my documents and told me to see him again when I have everything completed and he called in the next party that wanted to see him. I remembered that Baby Alalay, a former schoolmate at MIT, worked in the Building Department. I went to see her at her office and told her my predicament. All she could do was to whisper to my ear, "All those people on the front desks are corrupt. See what happens if you insert a fifty-peso bill in your roll of plans and make sure that he sees it." In 1976 the currency exchange was seven pesos to a dollar so fifty pesos was still a substantial amount.

I was flabbergasted. I knew that the Philippine government was so corrupt, but I did not expect that the day would come when I would personally be confronted with this anomaly. The situation got me thinking, what if I do what Baby Alalay suggested and I get charged with bribing a government official? I would be in big trouble, but I could not think of another alternative aside from fighting the system. How can one person, like me, fight the whole corrupt system? I knew they would gang up on me and make my life more miserable if I did. On the other hand, I did not really have any proof that such corruption was happening. All I knew was hearsay, such as what Baby Alalay alleged aside from all allegations I heard from radio and TV commentators and what I have read in newspapers. I made up my mind that I would like to see with my own eyes if these things were really happening. I inserted a fifty-peso bill on my rolled-up plans close to the end of the sheets. I decided that if the man turns out to be incorruptible, I will pretend that I had misplaced that fifty-peso bill, and I would thank him for helping me find it. So, I went on my own personal sting operation to witness for myself that corruption is indeed happening.

I waited till the man who rejected my construction documents was alone before I approached him again. I wanted to make sure that there would be no witness to my bribery attempt sting operation. I started to unroll my building plans making sure that he saw the fifty-peso bill I inserted between the sheets as I said, "there is one more question I would like to ask please."

Lo and behold, as soon as he saw the fifty-peso bill tucked conspicuously between the sheets of the building plans, the man took the roll of plans from me. He was immediately transformed into a friendly, helpful creature who immediately went on the process of reviewing my plans and he decided that my plans were in order, and he apologized for overlooking the details that were in the drawings after all. He started going about stamping my plans with all sorts of approvals while I looked at him condescendingly. I knew he would not look at me straight in the eye and I could not stop looking at him with disgust. What a leach, what a lowly creature, how can anyone sell his dignity for a mere fifty pesos. What a shame. I left the Building department with the building permit in my hand, but I was boiling mad inside with great feelings of indignity because I had become involved in corruption, and I have committed bribery. Was it really bribery? This corrupt official was so clever to maneuver an extortion to look like bribery on my part. I had witnessed firsthand how corruption was being perpetrated. I felt ashamed that I allowed myself to be part of it but if I did not witness it firsthand, I would not truly believe that these things were happening. If this kind of corruption was happening at this low level of government, I can imagine the kind of corruption going on in the higher level of government. It was so frustrating to be indignant about something but too cowardly to do anything about it. I admire people who courageously stand up for ideals they believe in undaunted by the consequences of their act and who dare to make a change. Unfortunately, I was not a hero material. I did not have the guts to go against a system that was overwhelmingly formidable to me. Aside from that, I had three little ones who were all dependent on me. I had to take all the precautions not to jeopardize my responsibilities as a mother. No wonder Ho Chi Minh stayed single and unattached.

The demeanor of the SSS employees gave me hope that there can be an establishment in the Philippines that can run cleanly without corruption. From my own observations I saw how every SSS employee graciously and cordially treated people that needed assistance with their SSS claims or benefits, very much unlike other Government offices I had observed in the past. Before I qualified to become an Instructor at the college level, I had to acquire some teaching course credits and get approvals from the Department of Education, and I was so disgusted at the way the government employees in that Department behaved. I was one of many, waiting for our turns to get assistance while the personnel who were supposed to attend to us took all their time doing things they were not supposed to do during working hours. I saw one woman who was supposed to attend to us took all her time freshening up her make-up in front of all of us. I happened to be with Dr. Pada, the Vice President of EARIST (Eulogio Amang Rodriguez Institute of Science and Technology) that employed me at that time. He was so kind to show me how to get my papers approved at the Department of Education because he also had to meet with someone at the Department and I was a newcomer to the education field who was completely at a loss at what to do. He got impatient with this lady at the counter freshening up her makeup and being a tall man, he reached over the 12"-high vertical glass panel over the counter and grabbed the make up kit from the lady's hand and authoritatively told her to do her duties first. Dr. Pada's tone made the lady oblige and I got my document processed. There was another time when I also saw one of these government employees selling some merchandise to another employee during working hours and they were all unconcerned about us waiting to be assisted. They wasted our time waiting and they all made us feel that we were at their mercy. I knew that if I started complaining I would be punished. They could make it harder for me to get my papers approved so I had to patiently wait until these government employees who feel that they were gods who were imposing their powers over a mere mortal like me, finally decided to attend to me. What an incompetent management, why wasn't there any Supervisor who saw to it that all employees did their jobs accordingly? Were they all waiting to be bribed before they would do something? No wonder, the Philippines is so unproductive.

I was proud to be an Appraiser for an organization that I believed to be incorruptible, and so I was having fun with my job. I was given three sites to inspect each day. I reported to the office in the morning to write up the report of the result of the inspection and based on my appraisal of the progress of the construction, I made the necessary calculations to determine my recommendation as to how much money should be released from the loan to finance the progress of the construction. However, if I had encountered any code violation or deviation from the approved plans, I would have to deny any release of the loan, partial or full, and notify the loan applicant in writing of the problem. There would be no further release of the money to finance the progress of the construction until the anomalies were rectified, or corrections were made, which were verified by another inspection. When a homeowner requested a first release of the loan, it was my duty to verify that the construction of the home was on the correct lot. The SSS held the title of the lot for the duration of the loan. Of course, since the amount of the loan was based on the value of the lot and the proposed building, it will be bad scenario if the house was constructed on a wrong lot and not where it was supposed to be. It was very important that I made sure the house was on the correct lot. This was easily verifiable when the whole block was already built-out but if the block was still empty of any structure, then I had to measure how far the construction site was from the corner of the block as indicated on the survey.

The professional way of ensuring that the house is erected on the correct lot is to hire a professional surveyor to stake out the building, but Filipinos always want to cut costs and the Building Department did not impose such procedures, so the responsibility was laid on the shoulders of us appraisers to make sure that the building was erected on the correct lot. It was very easy when the lot was a corner lot or up to four lots from the corner but when the lot was in the middle of the block more than a hundred meters away, that was when I got into complications. While I was a trainee, Fe helped me to determine my pace factor which was the average distance in meters of my pace. By multiplying my pace factor with the number of paces I made from the corner to the construction site I could determine the total distance. I was such a perfectionist I always had to pull the meter tape to be very accurate. Since my meter tape was only fifty meters long, I had to improvise a means of keeping the end of the tape securely in place before I started to pull it to the required length. There were times when I took Yayoy, my seven-year-old son, with me whenever he was free from school, so that he could hold the end of the tape. Other times I would have to look for a piece of rock to secure the end of the tape in place. There were several occasions when I had found constructions on the wrong lots; the worst one was a building being constructed right in the middle of two lots. Somehow a solution was always found to rectify this kind of problem. One solution was to find the owner of the lot where the construction was started and execute a lot swap if the lots were of identical sizes. We appraisers also strictly enforced ordinances of each Districts or Developments, making sure that the setback requirements were followed. I was very happy to enforce these restrictions because they prevented overcrowding and blight in any area.

When I started my field inspections, I measured all structural members to verify they were according to the approved plans but in time after repeated inspections I eventually learned to recognize the sizes of all structural members by sight. Just by looking I can distinguish a #3 reinforcing bar from a #4 or whatever size the bar is as well as timber structures, I learned to recognize by sight what a 2"×4" is or a 2"×6" or 2"×8" and so fort and so on. It would have been much easier for us appraisers if the Building Departments had been more competent and all we would require is a copy of inspection approvals from them whenever the homeowners requested releases of their loans. Unfortunately, none of the buildings I inspected went through any inspection by the Building Department.

Taxpayer money pays the salaries of Building Department officials, and the taxpayers are entitled to have the protection and assurance that their homes are being built soundly. Excavations for underground plumbing installations should not be back filled without the Building Inspector approval to ensure against any violation in plumbing connections and to ensure an efficient and smooth flowing plumbing system. Concrete foundations and slabs should not be poured until reinforcements are inspected and approved and likewise concrete columns and beams should not be poured until inspected and approved and so on and so forth, but I do not believe any of these were done by the Building Departments on any of the areas I was inspecting. Some Builders with enough capitals never requested releases of loans until the houses were already 100% completed and the full amount of the loans were released to them which meant that the houses were built purely by trust. If the Builder happened to be untrustworthy, no one would know until some calamity happens that would uncover whatever anomaly was committed. Who protects homeowners? Does anybody care? The designing Architect can provide the necessary inspections for an additional fee, but homeowners would not want to spend more than the design fee, so homeowners were not really clamoring for any protection so no one cared to scrutinize the incompetence of the Building Department. Perhaps these homeowners were afraid that if they demanded more protection their taxes would be raised, and Filipinos do not want to pay taxes and they would cheat whenever they could to pay less taxes. Also, more procedures in the system will give the corrupt government employees more reasons to extort taxpayers.

The SSSystem also provided vehicular conveyances for field inspection to the Real Estate Department. I always availed myself of a conveyance operated by an authorized driver whenever there was one available. Sites that were on distant locations were given priority. Brigido, whom we all called Brigitte was almost always my driver. He was such a gentleman and I always felt very safe with him. Brigitte and I had gone to so many far away inspections together and we had some quite unexpected surprises on several sites. One time I got a case file of a site somewhere in Central Luzon. It was more than a couple of hours trip one way. One of the Appraisers warned me to take care, "that is never-never land," he said. When we got on our way, I asked Brigitte, "What is never-never land?" He said, "That means NPA territory. Military men and Police officers would not dare go to those places because they will never be seen again."

"Is it safe for us to go there?" I asked, feeling a little weary.

"Don't worry. They know our Land Rover. They respect the SSS, they know we are helping them finance the construction of their homes." Our light-mossgreen-colored land rover had the insignia of SSS on its front, sides and rear and that gave me some assurance that nothing would go wrong because our vehicle would be easily recognized.

After driving for more than an hour on our way to never-never land, we came to a vast cornfield. It was so vast that we came to a point on the road where I looked back and I saw the road converged into a point where we came from and looking forward was the same thing, the road converged into a point where we were going, and this went on for kilometers upon kilometers of driving. There was no one else traversing the road during the whole length of the trip, and there was nothing else but corn stalks as far as the eyes can see everywhere. An eerie thought came to my mind. If ever some terrorists would suddenly come out of the corn stalks to ambush us, we were dead meat and there was no way we could get help from anyone. Mobile phones were not available for us in those days, and even if they were, there was no way help could have come on time. I tried to get this weary thought out of my mind by focusing on the landscape. It was so beautiful and peaceful. The field was no longer green but almost golden. The corn was all ripe and the field was ready for a bountiful harvest.

Never-never land was impressive. Although very modest, the whole community was very neat. The roads were lined with round river stones about a foot in diameter and painted white. The surroundings of each home were well maintained, and I did not see any kind of junk lying around anywhere. I saw a community of neat people who took the time to tidy and beautify their place with lovely colorful flowering plants. They must have had strong cooperation and they must have felt proud of their place. This was not typical of the poor communities I had seen which were usually foul smelling with dirty stinky trash seen scattered everywhere and buildings were neglected and dilapidated. The people I met were very cordial. This experience left a lasting impression in my mind. Was that what it meant to be an NPA? Perhaps they were trying to make a point. However, when I journeyed to another part of the Philippines years after my SSS employment, I heard tales of NPA abuses. One time, I went to visit a farmer and I noticed that there was enough space in his farm to raise cattle, so I ask him why he did not do so. I also noticed that the land could make more produce but instead it was just a waste land except for some meager plantings of vegetables, so I asked him why and his response was, "If I raise a cattle, the NPA would come and take it away and the same thing will happen if I plant more than what I can consume." Was he referring to thieves posing as NPA members or were those thieves truly members of the NPA? How can one tell?

NPA or National People's Army, a group of militants who are very unhappy about the Philippine government, wants to do to the Philippines what Ho Chi Minh did to Vietnam. Unfortunately for them, the Filipinos are not cohesive people, tribalism is still a strong inhibitor to attain cohesion, selfish people who are motivated only by their own personal benefits and they do not think in terms of what is good for the whole country. That is why the NPA movement will never amount to anything unless they produce a leader with the caliber of Ho Chi Minh who would be charismatic enough to create the cohesion necessary to bring all the people together to affect a change. But then again, the Americans would intervene in the guise of protecting democracy and there would be another bloody war. Who would want another bloody war? What the world needs is another charismatic leader like Mahatma Gandhi who would bring about change peacefully without resorting to violence. When I was taking a master's degree in Architecture at the University of the Philippines, I had a classmate who was very sympathetic to the NPA cause and I suspected that he was an active member. I wonder if he is still active in this anti-government movement, and I wonder what has become of him.

On another inspection to another far away site, Cavite, Southwest of Manila, Brigitte and I came upon the house of Mr. Bondoc who was requesting a final inspection. After a very long two-hour drive we came upon this property with a locked gate and there was no one in sight to let us in. Brigitte and I called out "Hello Mr. Bondoc on top of our lungs until our throats almost got sore and still no one came to see us. We were so frustrated that we drove for more than two hours for nothing. We were about to get back to the land rover when suddenly the main entry door of the house opened and a man who looked like a menial worker came to open the gate for us. We thought he would give us a tour of the house but instead; this man went towards the side fence, jumped over it and went inside the neighbor's house. Brigitte and I looked at each other with an unspoken, what's going on in here, question in our eyes. We were more surprised when the lady of the house, clad in a flush white bath robe emerged from the open door to greet us. Brigitte decided to wait in the Land Rover while the lady of the house let me in. Inside the dimly lit interiors of her home where all the windows were shut closed, a strong aroma of freshly sprayed room freshener greeted my nostrils. Brigitte always stayed in the land rover while I conducted my inspection, but I was sure that if he was with me that very moment, we would not have resisted giving each other a questioning glance.

The inspection went very well, the house was 100% complete, I did not have any problem recommending the final release of the loan. On our way home, I heard Brigitte say, "Poor Mr. Bondoc."

Yet on another inspection for a final release of the housing loan, I was given a tour of the newly constructed home by the homeowner who was so reluctant to let me in the bedroom. I explained to him that I cannot give 100% completion report without inspecting every room of the house, so he gave in and opened the bedroom door. The room was in perfect condition, but I saw a woman's clothing untidily hanging on the wall, which I surmised must belong to his wife and I wondered what his reluctance was about. When I opened the bathroom door I was surprised by the sight of a stark-naked woman, or I might even say a girl who looked too young to be the wife of the homeowner. She immediately tried to cover her nakedness with her hands in embarrassment. Oops! I gave her the chance to make herself decent before I went in the bathroom again for my final inspection. Why didn't the homeowner inform me right off that his wife wasn't decent in the bathroom? Made me wonder if there was some hanky-panky going on in the middle of the day.

There was a time that Brigitte and I braved a thunderstorm. While he waited for me in the land rover, I took cover under my umbrella hoping to keep dry in the downpour when a sudden blinding flash of lightning simultaneous with a deafening roar of thunder stopped my walk towards the house. My life must have been spared from being toasted by the lightning bolt by just a fraction of an inch because I was zapped by a jolt of electricity on my shoulder where the metal umbrella rod touched my skin. That was just one of the hazards of being an inspector out on the field. There was a time when I nearly fell off a roof in one of my inspections and there were several times that I bumped my head on scaffoldings because wearing a hard hat was not imposed. One other big problem of going on these far away field inspections was needing to have a bathroom break when there was no toilet available. Even if there was an out-house on the site, the stench would surely keep me away. Male appraisers would not find this kind of problems as difficult as female appraisers who are wearing pants during the field trip. That was one of my most dreaded predicaments. All constructions sites should be provided with portable toilets not just for us inspectors but for the construction workers as well.

Bringing presents for goodwill is a cultural thing among Filipinos or maybe among other people in other countries, like the Three Kings who brought presents for the baby in the manger. One time while I was on counter duty, I felt a sharp pointed moving creature prick my leg. I looked down under my desk to see a huge crab glaring at me. I was startled and I immediately jumped up to my feet. It was the biggest crab I have ever seen in my life with a body shell of probably a foot or more in length. One of the loan applicants brought a huge bag of live giant crabs as a goodwill present for an SSS employee and one of them got loose and started exploring our office. Fortunately, its claws were tied together, which prevented it from pinching anything.

Just as Fe had warned, I inspected several sites where homeowners or builders wanted to give me money. It seems that people on the third world countries have the mentality that bribery is the only way they can conduct business with the government or with any kind of business transaction for that matter or perhaps it is a cultural trait inherited from the past that people always bring tributes to win favors. I always felt degraded each time someone tried to give me gifts, which to me is bribery. I find it very demeaning for people to think that I can be bribed. One time, on the site of my first inspection for the day, a worker tried to hand me a twenty-peso bill. I told the man, "Please, you don't have to do that. I assure you that I am going to perform my duties accordingly without your gifts." On the second site on the same day, the construction was at a halt probably for lack of funds. There were no laborers on the site except for a man who tried to hand me another twenty-peso bill at the end of my inspection. I once again rejected it, but he was insistent. I took a taxicab on that day to conduct my inspections. As soon as I got inside the taxicab after completing all my inspections, he tossed the rolled-up money to me. I was really annoyed. Indignant, I grabbed the rolled-up money and flung it right out of the taxicab window. The guy was not looking so he probably thought I took the money, which made me angrier. I did not care anymore, and I told the taxi driver to proceed to the next site. As far as I was concerned, I had a clear conscience that I had kept my dignity and I knew that that money that I threw out of the taxicab window was lying out there among a heap of gravel on the site, finders' keepers!

The taxi fare was getting too expensive. I got off at the entrance of the subdivision and I decided to take a tricycle to the next site. The sun was blazing up in the sky, I was sweating like a dog, and I tripped and hurt my shin as I boarded the tricycle. It was one of those days where everything was going wrong, so I was not in my best mood when I got to my last site for inspection for the day. There was a man who was apparently waiting for me. After my inspection, this man handed me an envelope. I impatiently tore open the envelope and I found a fifty-peso bill with a note signed by Mr. Jose Mercado, the owner of the house being built, inside the envelope. The note was handwritten on a stationery with his printed letterhead, and it stated that he was hoping for a favorable recommendation. I went ballistic; that was the limit of my tolerance. "You guys are going to see what you're looking for," I thought, and with indignation, I left the site. I took the bribe envelope with the money and the note and on the following morning, I turned it over to Mr. Pineda, the RED Manager. Mr. Jose Mercado, the homeowner who gave me the note through the worker on the construction site was immediately summoned for questioning. He was charged with bribing a public official, his loan was in danger of being cancelled and all the money released to him would all be due and demandable. In the end, the decision to pursue the case against Mr. Mercado was left for me to decide because I was the key witness to his offense, but my soft heart prevailed, so I decided to drop the case. As far as I was concerned, Mr. Mercado had learned his lesson enough. A month later the SSS Administrator, Mr. Teodoro, gave me a commendation for honesty with a note conveying that he was pleased to hear a report of honesty instead of the usual negative reports of corruption.

After receiving my commendation for honesty, I started kind of feeling a little weird because the demeanor of the people I was working with at the RED had changed to being aloof. Were some people suddenly avoiding me or was it my imagination? I tried to convince myself that it was just my imagination, but I knew I was feeling some sort of body language from some of the employees that made me feel that they were avoiding me. Why should that be? Ignore it, just do your job, you are among people with dignity, I assured myself.

The SSS had a choral group, which I enthusiastically joined because I love to sing. Filo and Gogoy were members and through them I found out how I could join the group. Through the Choral group I became friends with employees from different departments. I learned from one of the Choral group members about Mrs. Vicente who was employed in one of the departments of SSS. Her family had a piano manufacturing business. I had always wanted to learn to play the piano, so I made arrangements with Mrs. Vicente to purchase an upright piano and pay on monthly installments until it was fully paid. Junn thought that a piano would only be a waste of money. He said it would only gather dust just like the piano in his parents' home. I ignored his objection. I wanted a piano, so I got one, I was paying for it anyway, which was also in retaliation for his on-going infidelity which I discovered very early in our marriage. When the piano was delivered to our home, all my three children, Yayoy, my oldest son who was already age seven at that time, Raqui age five and Tentong age four, wanted to play with it. My children's enthusiasm for the piano made me hire a piano teacher.

Beng was a seventeen-year-old music student at the University of the Philippines. She was the daughter of one of my Choral group friends. UP is very close to the SSS building and she would hang around during our choir rehearsals waiting for her Dad after school so they could go home together. She agreed to come every week to give lessons to my three little ones. All my three children learned very fast. I was very happy when I started hearing simple melodies from their tiny fingers. Yayoy was exceptional. He absorbed every new lesson like a sponge. One day, I heard Beng played Chopin's Nocturne. Yayoy heard this music piece for the first time, and he liked it and he asked Beng to teach the piece to him. Beng told him that Chopin's Nocturne was too advance for him. His fingers needed to grow longer to reach an octave. Yayoy would not be dissuaded so he learned the piece on his own, making his own improvisation by quickly moving his thumb and pinky to make it sound like he was playing the octave. For a seven-year-old to learn Chopin's nocturne on his own, to me was so exceptional. Junn also noticed the children's fast progress. He started to enjoy listening to them play. He always requested Yayoy to play Chopin's nocturne. I could tell that he knew he was wrong about disagreeing to buy the piano, but he was a person who would not want to admit that he was wrong. He is one of those guys who do not believe that his infidelity was wrong, and he used passages in the Old Testament of the Bible about the life of Abraham, to justify his womanizing. Anyway, I did not need to take piano lessons for myself anymore. I was quite satisfied listening to the children making music with the piano. I learn to play a few pieces on my own, like in two weeks I learned to play Beethoven's Fur Elise, but I easily forget because I do not practice enough.

We had athletic meets also at SSS and I was one of the players of the combined Real Estate Department and Accounting Department Volleyball team. These two departments were both on the fifth floor of the SSS building, RED was on the East end and the Accounting Department was on the West end. Our team uniform was a burgundy shirt with white trims and white shorts with burgundy trim. My brother Nonoy was commissioned to silk-print the team logo and player identification on the shirts. I had miniature uniforms made for my three little children so they could join me in our parade of athletes as mascots. Our team did not win the finals, but our performance wasn't too bad and what was important was that we all had great fun not only for us players but also for my three little children who enjoyed the athletic events with us.

Every year we had a wonderful Christmas Party at SSS. Each year someone got assigned to be chairman for this yearly event and when Filo and I were the chairmen, it was a big success. Christmas parties of previous years were nothing but luncheons for the entire staff, but Filo and I decided we would want a merrier celebration, so we organized a program. Filo and I being both members of the choir, sang 'Oh Holy Night' as a duet on our program. I also conducted some parlor games, which everyone enjoyed. One of the parlor games called REACT, which I introduced, became a tradition and we played it every Christmas party ever since. It was a game where all the different Sections of the RED were represented by a team of five players who were tested for their agility of mind and movement. The last team to react was eliminated until only one winner emerged as the victor over all other section teams of the department.

A week before Christmas we played Kris Kringle wherein, we chose a secret Kris Kringle pal by lottery, and we secretly made him or her happy with little presents everyday during the whole week until we revealed our identities to our secret Kris Kringle on our Christmas party where he or she reciprocated with a present. Each year, the Christmas party chairman tries to outdo the previous chairman in trying to make the party merrier from then on.

CHAPTER 5

Before My Days as an Appraiser

At home I had four maids, which is typical in Filipino households. There are so many young teenagers whose parents are too poor to support them, so they end up being domestic helpers or maids. I did not really need four maids, but I could not say no to them. My first maid was Delia who helped me take care of Yayoy while I worked to support our household because Junn was incapable of working at the start of my married life. He was recuperating from major lung surgery. Delia was such a nice 16-year-old girl who loved Yayoy as if he was her own baby. She broke down in tears when her mother took her away from my household to work in another home who promised a higher pay. Later, Naning, my young second-degree cousin was brought to my household by her mother, my mother's cousin. Then there was Virgie and then Marilyn. Then Nara, my neighbor's housemaid was fired and was thrown out on the street. Marilyn pleaded with me to take in Nara because she had nowhere else to go. Nara had physical abnormalities. She had a hunch back and one of her legs was shorter than the other, so she limped when she walked. I felt so sorry for Nara and I could not bear the thought of a young girl homeless out on the street, so I agreed to take her in. When I did that, my next-door neighbor got angry with me. She said she was only giving Nara a lesson. I persuaded Nara to go back to her previous employer and I explained to her that I did not want the ire of my neighbor, but Nara pleaded to stay with me, she said her former master was very abusive. My soft heart prevailed, and my neighbor never spoke to me again after that.

Nara in fact, replaced another maid who had just left. Marilyn told me that this other maid, whose name I could no longer remember, had been stealing from our food pantry to support her brother. Marilyn, who was so righteous, was adamant that she should be let go. Out of compassion, I could not ask this woman to leave because I understood that her desperation drove her to steal food to feed her hungry brother, but she left on her own, after Marilyn told her, "Ate knows what you're doing!". to make sure that she knew that I already knew that she had been stealing from me.

I treated all my maids, who all lived in my home, like my own sisters. There were advantages to having all four of them. The two little ones, Raqui and Tentong, were attending St. James Preschool and the oldest one, Yayoy, went to Claret school while I was working. Yayoy was picked up by the school bus while Virgie and Marilyn took Raqui and Tentong to the Preschool and waited until school classes were over. They enjoyed hanging around the school until Raqui and Tentong's classes were over because there were lots of other maids doing the same thing. They developed their own social circle. My maids had birthday parties at my home while my children and I conveniently disappeared in our Bedrooms. Anyway, I always put my children to bed at 7:00 every night and I read them stories until they all had fallen asleep. Junn never knew about my maid's birthday parties because he was never home early enough to see them. During these parties, my maids and their guests were always very well behaved and respectful of my presence even if I was not in sight. Whenever we went to the park, each of my three little children had an attending nanny who ran after them wherever they went. Going to the park was something we frequently did because my children loved to get on the swings and the slides and the seesaw and the parallel bars and play on the sand dunes and on all sorts of play apparatus available at the park. There were many times that after I came home from work, we brought our supper, which my maids had already prepared, to the park where we had frequent picnics. It was unfortunate that Junn could not join us all the time because of other more important things for him to do, more important than being with us.

My marriage to Junn had been stormy from day one. I must have loved him so dearly because I married him when he was so skinny, practically just skin and bones, even if I knew that he was a sick man. Or was it compassion that I felt for him because I knew he needed help and he needed someone to take care of him? I was completely influenced by the philosophy of life that Jesus admonished in my little book, The Imitation of Christ. The only endeavor that satisfied me was to look after the wellbeing of others. We both knew something was wrong with him because his x-ray showed a big tumor or whatever it was the size of a tennis ball on the lower end of his right lung. It must have been the reason why he could not gain any weight despite a good appetite for each meal. My naughty cousins called him ngepoy behind his back which was their slang for pangit, meaning ugly because he looked like a walking skeleton.

I met Junn when I was a graduating student at the Mapua Institute of Technology in Manila. The MIT Dean of the School of Architecture at that time was Dean Bondoc. He came to me to congratulate me for being the only scholar of the graduating class of the School of Architecture and Planning and he asked me to represent AR, short for School of Architecture, to the National Convention of the National Union of Students of the Philippines, held in Bacolod in 1965, Junn was the representative of the MIT School of Chemical Engineering, There were training sessions before the convention and Junn was among the leaders who was so impressive presiding over the training sessions. He was the president of the MIT Fraternity Theta Xi Epsilon. I must have intimidated AR students because although they showed me respect, none of them had shown any attention for me for any kind of romantic involvement. It didn't bother me at all because my policy is that a man must exceed my capabilities before I can consider him worthy of my attention to be my partner in life. There was a time that I heard one of my male classmates said to another, "How can I ask someone smarter than me for a date?" Was that meant for my ears? I wondered.

There were only 35 students in the AR graduating class that year and all our subjects were in the evening sessions because all of us were already working students and our Architectural Design Instructors were all practicing Architects. When my classmates started noticing the constant presence of Junn in the AR department, obviously because of me, they all connived to do a surprising stunt one night at the end of our design subject before we could all go home. As soon as our Instructor left our drafting room, to my surprise, they all hastily pushed three long tables where we lay our drafting boards at, around me forming a triangle, trapping me within. I was dumbfounded, I had no clue what their intention was for such a stunt. Everyone started to speak, one by one they voiced out their concern for me. All of them had nice things to say about me. I remember one saying, you are the marrying type and we had to be sure of our position in life before we could make decisions. Everyone disapproved of Junn to be my partner in life. They must have known more about Junn than me but at that time, I had no reason to push Junn out of my life. He was aspiring to be a Chemical engineer and his capabilities cannot be compared with mine and his excellent debating and leadership capabilities that he displayed during our training sessions for the convention were beyond compare. What my classmates did showed me what I meant to all of them, and I appreciate it very much to this day.

After graduating at the Mapua Institute of Technology with a Bachelor of Science degree in Architecture, one of my Instructors, Architect Aquilles Paredes recommended me to be the assistant of a lady Architect, Aida Cruz who made a career name for herself in Baquio City. She married Jose del Rosario who became the General Manager of the Iligan Integrated Steel Mills in Iligan, on the island of Mindanao. I graduated ahead of Junn at MIT so while he was finishing his Chemical Engineering course, I accepted the position of becoming the assistant of Aida Cruz del Rosario in Iligan City until Junn graduated from MIT after six months, so as not to be a distraction to him to finish his college degree. I did not intend to work longer than six months in Iligan because I was too far away from my loved ones, especially my family. It was the very first time in my life to be away from my family.

I got along very well with the del Rosario family, specially their three youngest children who were in grade school. One by one the three little ones started to sleep with me in my bedroom until all of them were with me every night sleeping with me in a queen-size bed. I did not have a clue that the three little del Rosarios were a preview of my own Yayoy, Raqui and Tentong in my future. I went home for Christmas, and I was so happy to back with my family and I told Aida that I was too lonesome to be away from my family that I would like to end my employment with her but Jose del Rosario made an offer to Junn to work as a quality control technician at IISMI so that I can continue to work as Aida's assistant. I asked Mr. del Rosario if there were any qualifying examinations that Junn had to take and his reply was, "Just the physical exams". And so, Junn went to have his x-ray taken and that was how we discovered the mysterious big black round thing he had been carrying in his chest for the past six years.

While waiting for Engineer Del Rosario's confirmation of Junn's employment at IISMI, Mama told us, "If you two are going to Iligan together, you better get married first." All right Mama. On the 11th of May 1968, Junn and I went in front of Father Robles at the Project 6 Catholic church to say our "I do's" without much ado, wearing our church clothes, no wedding gown, no marching down the aisle and Mama lent us her ring for the ceremony, we didn't even have proper wedding rings. I had to return the ring to Mama after the ceremony. We all went to a restaurant for dinner afterwards with Mama and Apang (that's how my siblings and I called our beloved father) and all my brothers and sisters and Junn's relatives. I was the first to marry among my siblings, ahead of my older sister Mila. During the ceremony, I looked at the attendees of our wedding and I saw Apang in tears, as if he had foreboding feelings about my marriage.

The IISMI Doctors examined Junn's x-rays and they decided that he would be an employment risk for the IISMI company so the whole idea of working in Mindanao was scratched off.

It took six months after we got married before Junn finally agreed to get confined at Quezon Institute, a hospital in Quezon City that specialize in lung ailments. Manuel Quezon was the Philippine President during the Second World War who died of tuberculosis. Quezon Institute was established in commemoration for him. Junn's family was not supportive of the idea of having him confined at Q.I. because it had the stigma of being the home of tuberculous people and people fear getting close to one sick of TB. Their concern was understandable since TB bacteria can be airborne and you can get it if you breathe it into your lungs. I knew Quezon Institute was the best place to go for lung ailment so as soon as we got married, I went to see Dr. Marfil a family acquaintance who was a principal doctor at the Institute and who was a fellow physician of Dr. San Pedro. We came to know Dr. Marfil because the sister of my auntie Gene, the wife of Mama's younger brother Jose, was a nurse at QI. As soon as Dr. Marfil saw Junn's x-ray, she told me right away that my husband needed to get to the hospital for observation and treatment. Junn would not heed my pleadings for him to go to the hospital. He had just gotten employed with Metro Oil where his older brother Tony was employed, and he did not believe he had any physical affliction. He was not feeling any symptoms except that he was so skinny, so he was ignoring the x-ray results. Weight loss is a symptom of something, but he did not care to find out why he was not gaining weight. Was he fearful of facing the truth?

Mamang could not admit that there was something wrong with her son either, "His doctor said that his ailment had calcified, maybe that big round thing on his lung is how calcified looks like in x-ray," she argued.

That big round thing as big as a tennis ball lodged on his son's lung had to be examined. That was what the doctor said, and I believed what the doctor said. That was when I found out that Junn had been to Q.I. before when he was only eighteen years old. Q.I. had his medical history. His lady doctor, Dr. San Pedro, diagnosed that he had flurisy, or water of the lungs. She recommended a procedure where a needle would be inserted through his side into his lung to drain the water out. His mother got scared of Dr. San Pedro's diagnosis. No way was she going to allow any doctor to puncture her son's lungs. She went for a second opinion to another doctor who was not a lung specialist who assured her that Junn's condition had calcified and that he did not need to be punctured by a fearsome needle. This incompetent doctor's diagnosis was what Mamang decided to believe, it saved her a lot of money on what she believed to be "unnecessary medical procedure". So, seven years later Junn's x-ray showed like he had swallowed a tennis ball that had lodged on his lungs because the water on his lungs had already turned to puss and this time pricking him with a needle would not do anything anymore.

Junn's employment with Metro Oil lasted only for a couple of months. He would not tell me why but from overhearing his conversation with Tony, his older brother, and his other fraternity brothers whose friendly ties with him stayed very strong, I could deduce that he had failed to turn in his money collection to the company. He was entrusted with some cash at Metro Oil. He was newly employed. Could he have embezzled funds as soon as he was entrusted with cash? I could not believe it. He was a very respectable and responsible Theta Xi Epsilon Fraternity President in college. I was very impressed with the way he presided over the meetings and the very responsible manner he carried out his presidency. I expected him to be a very responsible employee and husband as well. Junn did not want to talk about the reason he lost his job at Metro Oil and I did not bother to pursue the subject because he needed to be physically examined to clarify what was in his x-ray films anyway.

Maybe it was a blessing in disguise; maybe it was for the best that he lost his job. He needed to go to the hospital anyway. But Junn still could not be persuaded to go to the hospital. If only I could get his family's backing to persuade him, but they were not supportive of my concerns at all. I was the only one pushing him to get treated. He found another job with Dow Corning to do research work. His employment again lasted for only a few months because he made the mistake of mentioning Metro Oil in his employment history. He thought Dow Corning would not bother to find out about his performance with Metro Oil. Apparently, he was wrong. I heard Tony say to him, "Don't mention Metro Oil in your application again, brad," when we went bowling with him one time, which we frequently did those days.

Once again, he was out of a job. He finally conceded to go to the hospital. I went back to Dr. Marfil to tell her that Junn finally agreed to be confined. In November of 1968, Junn and I went to Quezon Institute. Dr. San Pedro, his doctor seven years earlier, was there to greet him when we stepped in the Admission Office. She greeted Junn, "Well Mr. Villanueva, long time no see. Are you sure you would go through the procedure this time? Or would you want to wait another six years when you would be like this," with sarcasm she mimicked someone hard of breathing and in the verge of dying, "By that time we won't be able to help you anymore," she added. I could tell her deep regret that Mamang ignored her recommendation seven years ago. I saw her shake her head gently sideways in frustrated resignation as she walked away. Her frustration is understandable because a very simple procedure could have prevented what turned out to be very invasive surgery.

It was so heart breaking leaving Junn in the hospital. I was sobbing all the way home, I felt so sorry for him and at the same time I felt so sad and lonely that we would be away from each other during his confinement, but he had to be medically treated. It had to be done. Every night after work I visited Junn. He had made several friends in the ward after being there for a few weeks. I remember making a paper sculpture of the Nativity scene to brighten up their ward when Christmas season drew near. He would request a box of KFC sometimes so I would stop at the take-out counter of the restaurant before I went to see him. On weekends he was allowed to go home. I picked him up on Fridays after work and accompanied him back to the hospital on Monday mornings. I did not see any of his relatives visiting him during the month-long observation period, but I did not bother to ask Junn, I did not want to know the answer. Perhaps they had come during the daytime while I was working.

Junn went through a series of tests and examinations and finally his biopsy confirmed the results. The verdict of his Surgeon, Dr. Jesus de Jesus who was called Dr. JJ for short, was lobectory. His lowest right lung lobe had to be cut off because the infection was already spreading to the middle lobe, which already needed decortication. Junn and I were devastated by the verdict, but we did not have any choice because if the procedures were not done immediately, instead of a lobectomy with only the lowest lobe being ectomized, it would be pneumoectomy, the whole right lung would soon have to go. It boggled my mind to know that it was a procedure that could have been prevented had his mother consented to the recommendations of Dr. San Pedro. How could a well-educated woman, with a masters degree in Education from the University of the Philippines, awarded teacher of the year, author of a textbook for chemistry in high school, made such a decision? Now her son had to go through major surgery because of her choice. His right side had to be cut wide open and one of his rib bones was removed to give ample room for Dr. JJ's hand to work on this serious operation instead of a tiny needle going through his side. I tried to console myself with the thought that he was more fortunate than his roommate in the recovery room at the hospital who had one of his lungs completely removed.

Junn roomed with a handsome young man at the men's ward at QI who successfully went through a pneumoectomy but on Valentine's Day, just about a few days over a month after his surgery, his girlfriend broke up with him. The poor man was already severely depressed by the fact that he had lost a lung, the added heartache for loosing the woman he loved was too much for him to bear. He jumped out of his window from the second floor; his surgical wound was still very fresh. He suffered massive hemorrhage and died. The doctors could not stop his bleeding. I came on the night the tragedy happened and I found all the patients still in shock because of the tragic event. I was shocked myself and I felt deeply sorry for the poor young man. How can that woman be so utterly heartless? She could have waited till the poor man had recuperated. It was exactly a month after Junn had his surgery. He was still recuperating, and I worried that it would affect him. Shortly afterwards, I realized that it did because he was a changed man when he came out of the hospital.

Dr. JJ gave us a choice whether Junn would have the surgery before or after Christmas and we chose to spend Christmas together at home and that was when I conceived for Yayoy, my first baby. His surgery was performed at eight in the morning of January 14, 1969, which lasted five hours. Every night after work I went to the hospital to help nurse Junn get back to health. I was almost twenty-five years old at that time, pregnant, and working as hard as I could to support both of us and our baby who would soon be born. We did not have any medical insurance and I was the only one working. I had to pay all the medical bills. The family of his roommate who jumped out of the window paid ten thousand pesos for the operation. Where in the world would I get that kind of money? It would take me a lifetime to pay off that kind of medical bill.

Dr. Marfil, a very kindhearted lady doctor at the hospital, saw my predicament right from the beginning. She made arrangements so that Junn would stay at the charity ward during his confinement. I had to pay all medications and the Doctor's bill and the blood that was needed for his major surgery. I tried to ask for help from his family. He was already sick when I married him, but his family was unwilling to help. I could not believe that they were really unable to help because the Villanuevas had material assets to their name, they own their own home, and they had a car, and I did not have anything except for my ability to work and get substantial enough income to get through the predicament. For a Filipino to own a home and a car means he has assets. I am sure they had cash assets too. Did they see that I was there anyway who was willing to shoulder the financial burden of Junn's medical needs? Why would they part with their assets if they didn't have to? Dr, JJ told me that Junn needed 3,000cc of blood for the surgery. The doctors would not take blood from me because I was underweight. I thought that his father and mother and three brothers could donate blood for him, but Mamang was scared that they would get sick too if they gave blood. They donated blood to the Red Cross, but they were too scared to donate for the needs of their own son and brother. They donated blood to the Red Cross and they gave me all their Red Cross donor cards because donors were supposed to be entitled to free blood when they are in need but I quickly found out that you need to know somebody at the Philippine Red Cross before you can avail of any help or perhaps they wanted some bribe money before they would give me the amount of blood that Junn needed?. I was flatly denied the much-needed blood despite all the donor cards that I presented to them, not a single drop was available. Their excuse was that they did not have any in stock. I had to pay for every milliliter of blood that was transfused to Junn's arteries.

I knew Junn's parents could have helped but they chose to put the entire financial burden on my shoulder because that was the way they were. Mamang was not convinced that his son needed that kind of surgery until she watched the operation from the viewing room above the surgery room. It was only then that she offered to pay the operating room fee but every little prescription for medications that Dr. JJ handed to her, she handed to me. Dr. JJ probably thought that Junn's parents were the ones shouldering all the medical expenses because he knew we were newlyweds, and I was only twenty four years old.

Before Junn went to the hospital, we lived with his parents. There was constant bickering between Mamang and Papang, Junn's parents. Papang was always drunk and when he got drunk, he would be transformed from a henpecked husband into a real screaming monster who terrorized everybody. I moved back to my parent's home as soon as Junn went to the hospital, but we would go to his parent's home on weekends when Junn was allowed weekend leave from his hospital confinement. I could not stand the daily bickering at the Villanueva household. I knew that as soon as Junn got out of the hospital, I would have to live in his parents' home again and I could not allow that to happen ever again.

I worked as a draftsman for an Interior Designer, Nestor de Castro from 1965 while I was still an Architectural student at Mapua Institute of Technology. It was also my Instructor, Aquilles Paredes, who recommended me to Nestor. Nestor shared the office with his Architect brother, Cresenciano de Castro. One time, Cresenciano, whom everyone called Eseng, was trying to meet a deadline to finish the plans for the home of a very important client. He asked Nestor if he could borrow my services to help in the Architectural department. What started as a temporary arrangement became a permanent one. Nestor repeatedly asked Eseng when I would be doing Interior Design work for him again but apparently Eseng being the older brother had the upper hand. I became part of the CCCastro and Associates Architectural staff until I left Manila to work for Aida Cruz del Rosario for six months in Mindanao. When our plan to work in Iligan did not materialize, I went back to CCCastro and Associates. The Company embarked on an exciting venture to compete against the top Filipino Architects in a very prestigious Architectural Competition aimed in designing the Asian Development Bank and United Nation Complex in Manila. All drawings of the Plans, Elevations and Cross Sections of the building complex were to be hand drawn in pen and ink on 20"×36" Illustration boards and that was one of my expertises. I was a top pen and ink delineator and CCCastro and Associates gladly gave me back my position in their firm. This was the late sixties, a time when computer generated drawings were not yet available in Manila. With my employment with CCCastro and Associates I managed to financially cope with the responsibilities on my shoulders.

Very close to my parent's apartment, I saw the groundbreaking for the construction of a new apartment. I immediately went to see the owner, Mrs. Burog, my parent's neighbor, and paid a month's rent in advance to reserve one unit for me. It was a very small two-bedroom apartment, just a few steps from my parents' home and for me it was perfect. Mama was adamant when she heard of what I did. "Have you gone mad? Your husband is sick, and you committed yourself to a monthly rent expense that you don't need. That's like picking up a stone and hitting your own head with it. Do you know what it means to pay rent every month? Go and tell Mrs. Burog that you are canceling," she demanded. I did not say a thing, it was pointless to argue.

A month before Junn came home, I moved to my newly constructed apartment. I did not have any furniture except a bed. Mama allowed me to take my old bed with me when she realized there was nothing that could stop me from moving. She also gave me her small breakfast table with matching two chairs. She bought a new range, and she gave me her old tabletop burners for cooking. She also bought a new refrigerator so that I can have her old one, which had gotten too small for her and my dad and growing brothers and sisters anyway. She could not bear to see me living in my apartment all alone, so she told Anita, my younger sister, to stay with me so we moved Anita's bed to the other bedroom of my apartment. Anita was a nursing student at the University of the Philippines at that time and she moved out when she started her nurse training at the Philippine General Hospital to stay at the dormitory. As soon as her training was over, American agents recruited her among nine other fellow nurses who all graduated together from the same class to work in the United States. She left in 1974.

All the stresses of having Junn go through the necessary medical procedures added to my exposure to the tuberculous patients in the hospital plus all the havoc that my pregnancy was causing in my body weakened my own health and my pregnancy was threatened. It was a very difficult pregnancy and I felt sick the whole day. One day, I coughed out blood and I immediately consulted Dr. Marfil and she advised me to go straight home from work and rest from then on, otherwise I could lose my baby. She assured me that Junn was already out of danger. At that time, I could not afford a telephone connection so I could not communicate with Junn during the week, but I visited him on weekends for the remaining couple of weeks of his stay in the hospital. The fact that I could not see him everyday anymore must have had a devastating effect on Junn. At the height of our marital problems eight years later, he lashed out to me, "where were you when I needed you!" Wasn't he told that I coughed out blood and needed rest myself?

Junn came home from the hospital two months after his surgery to our new apartment. Mamang came to visit and saw our empty living room. She came back with a truck loaded with her old wooden living room set that had caned seats and backrests. She also got us a telephone connection. Our apartment was finally fully furnished with hand me downs. I was not making enough to afford a television set, but I was content, I had everything I needed. I borrowed my mother's sewing machine and, in the evening, I started sewing clothes for the ladies in our neighborhood to supplement my income from my employment at Architect Eseng's office. I had learned to sew from my Home Economics class in high school when I was only fourteen and I had been sewing my own clothes since then. I was happy to discover that I was a very good dressmaker. I had a good sense of proportion needed for designing clothes and I drafted the patterns of my own designs. I was able to make a lot of women happy with my sewing. Some of them came every week for a new dress. My list of customers grew from word of mouth.

Junn recovered very well but for reasons I could not understand at that time, I noticed that he was no longer the same man I had married. He was so quiet, lying down in bed day and night, hardly talking to me. He used to be so loving and full of fun and in fact very possessive. He used to be the jealous type who would look for telltale evidence in my purse and would want to know who was on the bus with me when he found two bus tickets in my purse with consecutive numbers. I had a hard time assuring him that it was my sister who was on the bus with me. Before he got confined at the hospital, he would sometimes unexpectedly appear at Architect Eseng's office and waited for me till work was over. He would subject me into intense interrogation when I happen to walk out of the office at the end of the day with a male office mate, which was almost always the case since I was the only lady draftsman at that time.

His possessiveness had gotten to a point that it was beginning to annoy me, how can he distrust me, me who was such a strict follower of rules specially God's laws.

He stayed in bed day and night to recover fully. After a few months of inactivity, I thought that it would be better for him to start stretching his bones. I was also getting frustrated that I was already eight months pregnant, and he still could not even help me carry the garbage out to the street for pick up. There was a time that out of frustration I told him, "you lazy bone!" I regret having said it, but I guess I was just another human being in need of some kind of moral and physical support for all the hardships I was going through. Things were getting bad, my pregnancy made me feel sick the whole day. I had a molar that bothered me with relentless pounding pain the whole length of my pregnancy, but I was too scared to take any pain killer fearing that it would have a bad effect on my baby in my womb. Those were the days when tales about thalidomide babies were still in the news. We both needed some kind of support but we both were emotionally incapable of helping each other.

Seven months after his surgery, a month before my baby was born, Junn finally got employed at the Alhambra Industries. It did not take long after he got employed before he started coming home late. On the night I needed to go to the hospital to have my baby, Junn, could not be found. Mama and my cousin Nympha were the ones who took me to the hospital. During the three nights that I was in the hospital, Junn showed up only once. He did the same thing when my two other babies were born.

The hour he came home from work got later and later until he was coming home in the wee hours of the morning. "I was with the boys," was his excuse. While we were in college, I had seen how close he was with his fraternity brothers and every time he said he was with the boys I assumed he meant he was with his fraternity brothers. I would tell him to come home early, and I would prepare a sumptuous dinner for him, but dinner got cold and there was no Junn. I waited and waited every night for my husband to come home before I went to bed but he never came home before midnight. I did all sorts of things while waiting for him, sew one more dress for a customer or did some crocheting or read a book till midnight but he never came while I was awake. One very late evening, I was crocheting a dress when Mama and Apang, my Mom and Dad, came by my window and with a very concerned voice I heard Mama said, "Pura, go to sleep, it's almost midnight." They were on their way walking home from a mahjong session at my Auntie Ome, nickname for Salome, whose home was just a block away. After that I waited for my husband after nine in the evening in the dark because I did not want my parents to worry for me. They regularly went to Aunt Salome's mahjong sessions for fun, and they always passed by my apartment on their way home. After countless nights waiting in the dark, I learned to go to bed alone. I had a little baby to look after; I could not afford to get sick.

One weekend, Junn came home with Celso Liceralde, one of his fraternity brothers whom I had met while we were in college. Celso was very much against marital infidelity. During his visit, he told Junn, "You have to stop this affair you are having with your mistress. Your wife needs to know about it, and you have to put an end to it." I could not believe what I heard. It could not be true after all we've been through. I was shocked and terribly hurt. Junn was apologetic, or was he putting on the act in front of Celso's presence? He asked me how I would want him to prove that the affair was over. I told him, "I want to meet your woman. I want her to know that you are a married man."

A week later, I was surprised by the visit of a woman who brought a rubber ball for a present for my Yayoy who was then about a year and a half old. She introduced herself as Remy. She came because she wanted to prove to herself that Junn was indeed married. She said that she could not believe that Junn had a family because ever since they met, they had spent every single night together. I asked her how long the affair had been going on. She said over a year and a half, which meant the affair started as soon as Junn got employed at Alhambra Industries. She promised that she would not see Junn ever again, but I knew that it was a hollow promise. Remy's appearance in my home proved to me that Junn was trying to make amends but if he was, how come he never came home right after work? He continued to come home at dawn everyday. He continued to deny the affair was still going on and insisted that he was with the boys again. I was married and yet I was alone. In the Philippines there is no divorce. What can a woman like me do?

I was four months pregnant with my daughter Raqui when Remy came to visit. I did not want to have a third child after my daughter was born but Junn wanted to prove his power over me. I had another son exactly a year and a day after my Raqui was born. My first son Yayoy was born on September 10, 1969, my daughter Raqui was born on September 11, 1971, and my youngest son Tentong was born on September 12, 1972. I love all three of them so dearly. They gave me a purpose for my otherwise useless existence. Since their birthdays were on three consecutive days, each year we had only one birthday party. We had one huge birthday cake for the yearly party. On one birthday party, one corner of the cake had seven candles for Yayoy, another corner had five candles for Raqui and another corner had four candles for Tentong. They blew their candles all together at the same time.

When Yayoy was six months old, I came home one day from work to find my baby unusually lethargic while awake and not the usual bundle of fun who was so full of energy and when I picked him up from the crib, he was so limp. I was so alarmed, and I asked Delia, the sixteen-year-old girl who took care of Yayoy while I was working, what happened. Delia told me that Yayoy had been having diarrhea the whole day. I immediately bundled up my baby and walked to Dr. Oliveros who conducted her medical practice at her home just a block away. My baby was already suffering from dehydration, but Dr. Oliverous assured me that he would be all right. The kind lady doctor instructed me how to properly nourish my baby in his condition and she prescribed whatever medication was needed. This incident made me decide to quit my work with Architect Eseng where a very disappointing thing happened anyway, which drained all my enthusiasm for my architectural work at his firm. I decided to devote the whole day sewing clothes for my lady customers so that I could watch my baby closely. Some of my customers did not know that a licensed Architect was sewing clothes for them. They probably would not understand how I could give up such a prestigious position to become a lowly dressmaker, which in the Philippines was not given high regard because Filipinos do not respect labor, which was unfortunate. Filipinos looked down on laborers. This is why labor is dirt cheap in the Philippines. It was a derogatory thing to be known dating a chimay, their slang for housemaid. This is another legacy of Spanish colonization.

Motherhood for me was a priority above my career. I did not care what other people thought. While sewing for my customers, I could stay at home and supervise the development of all my three babies. I employed Delia, who was my first live-in household helper to look after Yayoy so that I could continue working at CCCastro and Associates. She helped me take care of Yayoy while I worked at the Architectural office and at night, I started sewing clothes for my customers to supplement my office income since I was the sole bread earner while Junn was still incapable of working for a living. Delia became so attached to Yayoy. She was in tears when the time came when her mother took her away from us without giving me any reason, but I suspected that she would transfer her to the home of another employer who would pay her a higher monthly wage. I would have agreed to negotiate with her, but she did not give me any chance. Delia gave Yayoy a big hug and sobbed bitterly before she finally said goodbye. Poor Delia, she was her mother's slave, it was her mother who collected her monthly income. I didn't approve of it but Delia was so subservient to her mother that she handed her wages to her every month.

I felt so sorry for those young girls who worked as household helpers who were practically slaves of their own parents. Their parents dictated where they would work, determined by whichever household would give them the highest wage. I had seen cases where some of these parents would collect the wage of their daughters for as much as three months in advance and these poor girls worked to pay off the money their parents collected in complete obedience without any complaint, they themselves getting nothing. Delia was one of those girls who obediently followed whatever her mother wanted her to do. She and others like her had been brainwashed into thinking that they owe their lives to their parents, so they must obey whatever their parents decided for them. They were practically slaves of their own parents. When they got married and had children, they treated their children the same way. I do not know how long this unfortunate tradition has been passed on from one generation down to the next, but I am sure that this is an outcome of the desperation stemming out of poverty. I wish I could do something to change this mentality, but I do not know how.

In three years, I had three babies. I continued to be a seamstress while Junn continued his philandering. Occasionally I got commissions to design private homes or apartment buildings which I did on my own at home and these few projects kept me practicing my true profession. We had moved to a bigger apartment. My older sister Mila and her family moved to a bigger home. She and her husband Mo rented their apartment to me, which was also on the same block where my parent's home was, so we were not really going too far away from my Mama and Apang's place, just a few more steps farther. Also, Mila and Mo's apartment was on a business section of the block, on Road 1, the main road entering the housing community. My dress shop could be in full operation with a display window right there on the main road. I bought the prettiest mannequin I could find. I started hiring seamstresses too and I had three household helpers. Yayoy and Raqui adjusted very well on their new home because they had been there many times before playing with their cousins Marco and Moca. It took Tentong who was just a year old a little longer time to adjust. My maids and I had to take turn carrying him around until he got adjusted to his new surroundings.

A year after we got settled in our new apartment, my cousin Ding who lives across the street came by to visit. In a roundabout way he insinuated to me that Junn was still seeing someone. He did not know that I had met Remy already and I presumed he was referring to her. He could not say it straight out, but I got the message. I was beside myself, completely outraged. It was the weekend before Easter. I told my maids that I would disappear for the weekend to calm myself down and told them to take care of the children. I needed to be alone for a couple of days for my nerves to settle down. The frustrations and disappointments of my marriage had become unbearable. I was actually lost and I really did not know what else to do. I was hoping that a religious retreat would help me sort out my problems with Junn. I did not tell anyone where I was going. I saw an Ad for a close retreat for a very affordable price in a nunnery not too far away. I packed what I needed for the close retreat for Catholic women and left.

At the retreat house, I found a Priest who was willing to talk to me and confiding my emotional turmoil to him was a big help. It always helps to be able to vent out your grievances to sympathetic ears. At the end of the retreat, the kindly Priest suggested to me to give Junn a call and to ask him to pick me up so he would know why I disappeared. Junn came. He had a short talk with the Priest. I did not know what the Priest told him and whatever it was it soon became apparent that Junn was determined that he would not change his ways.

It was Holy Week, 1974. President Marcos had declared the whole week as a holiday. All offices were closed but Junn would not stay home. Why was he punishing me? Why was he tormenting me? Junn's depraved indifference was crushing me, and it had taken a toll on my spirit. There was a great upheaval down deep inside me that was wanting to explode. I grabbed my purse and ran out of our apartment and took a bus for Luneta Park at the Manila Bay. I had been crying and my eyes were puffy from too much crying. I got off the bus and I found myself walking towards the seawall by the bay, at that time, it was still the way it was when our National hero Rizal was executed by the Spanish tyrants, where you can watch the glorious sunset at Manila Bay. I sat on the seawall to feel the soothing ocean breeze on my face, on my body, on my whole being. Watching the glorious sunset and the undulating rhythm of the waves wildly crashing into the rocks beneath the seawall breaking up into foamy rivulets playfully finding their way back to the sea pacified my tormented mind and my aching heart. This was before the despicable reclamation project in Manila happened when Luneta Park was still right on Manila Bay, which is now destroyed by the reclamation projects of the despicable Filipino oligarch who destroyed this beautiful historic landmark to erect their high-rise building complex that benefit them alone and enrich their pockets. All Filipinos were robbed of the wondrous exhilarating experience of watching the glorious sunset at the Manila Bay that was lost forever.

The upheaval within me subsided. It was then that I became aware of a presence on my right side a couple of meters away, so I turned to look. I saw a Caucasian foreigner also watching the glorious sunset seated at the seawall and he winked at me when our eyes met. I winked back to him and after a few moments of hesitation we started talking to each other. I normally would ignore a stranger's wink but my frustrations and disappointment with my life made me wink back at him. We started a conversation. I found out that he was Wolfgang Mecicer from Milan, Italy, born on the 1st of May 1945 so he was about a year younger than me. He was in Manila for business reasons. He was not expecting that the whole week would be declared a holiday. He had to wait for a week to perform his business transactions.

Before coming to the Philippines, he stopped at Japan. He said Japanese people were stupid and yet he was apparently very impressed with the Japanese camera that he had bought. It seemed to me that he was wearing a Japanese wristwatch as well. I got the impression that he was annoyed by the Japanese people because they could not speak English as good as Filipinos do. Communication with them must have been difficult, that was why he called them stupid.

Wolfgang was a tall, good looking blond man with deep blue eyes, well mannered and I enjoyed my conversation with him very much. He invited me for a drink at the cocktail lounge of the hotel where he was staying. I had never accepted an invitation from a stranger before, but he looked like a trustworthy man, and I was already so fed up with the way my life was going so I agreed. The hotel where he was staying was walking distance from the park because Luneta was on the tourist belt of Manila. While we were walking, he asked." Tell me why you had been crying."

"You wouldn't want to know. You might end up crying too." was my reply.

We continued to walk, and we came by some art galleries on our way, "What do you do?" He asked.

"I'm a painter," I lied while looking at the paintings at the gallery. It was not completely a lie. I had done some oil paintings in my leisure time.

"What do you do with your paintings?"

"I give them away." I could never be a good liar. I knew my response was not very convincing.

When we got to his Hotel, he made some arrangements with the gentleman at the front desk and then he led me to the elevator. I was thinking, maybe the cocktail lounge is on the rooftop? The elevator stopped midway to the top and he led me out to the hallway. We ended up in his room. I started to get uneasy. He asked me to have a seat and make myself comfortable and then he excused himself because he had to make a telephone call and his hotel room did not have one. He was gone for a short while and when he reappeared, he jumped on the bed and bade me to join him. His invitation looked so innocent, so I joined him in his bed in an innocent cuddle with my back towards him. He was so comforting. It was exactly what I needed at that time. I needed a good hug so badly it felt like Wolfgang was Jesus Christ who came in person to comfort me, after all, all the images of how Jesus Christ was typically portrayed was very much like him with beard and mustache added.

The hair on his skin fascinated me. It was my first very close encounter with a blonde person, and to me all the strands of hair growing on his skin looked like gold. "Your hair looks like gold," I said.

"I should shake them all off, and I shall be rich," he jokingly replied.

After a long pause he asked. "Have you known a man?"

Why did he ask me that question, "No," I again lied. It would be safer for me to make him think I was a virgin, I thought. He made a little move that made my whole-body tense up and I am sure that my body language conveyed to him that I was serious about not getting into any kind of intimacy. I could have done something to spite Junn right then and there but every fiber in my body would never allow me to break the law, either the law of man or more importantly, the law of God. I was sure that Wolfgang would never do anything against my will, and I knew I was safe in his company.

We rested for a bit more and then he got up and told me that he had to call Milan to tell them about the unexpected weeklong holiday in the Philippines. He asked me to wait for him. His errand did not take long. As soon as he came back, he said, "Let's have that drink I promised you."

Before we left his room, he gave me a brotherly kiss on my forehead and he spoke, "If my friends hear about this, they will think I'm stupid."

His comment made me smile. It was so refreshing to be with a true honorable gentleman who was so good looking and intelligent too.

The cocktail lounge was on the ground floor. I asked for a glass of orange juice. His business connection, a couple of gentlemen with a lady friend arrived while we were having our drinks. He did not tell me that he was waiting for these people; planning to meet with them must have been the first telephone call that he made while I waited in his room. I then realized why we had to wait for a little while in his room. The newcomers proposed going to a nightclub for some dancing and they invited me to come along. I declined the invitation, and I told them that I did not want to go with them because I was not properly dressed. I was wearing a pair of blue jeans; an old faded blue shirt and I was wearing my house slippers plus I was a married woman with three children who according to our society's morals was not supposed to do those kinds of things. But Wolfgang stretched out his arms to his sides and looked down at his own outfit which was denim pants, denim shirt and leather sandals on his feet, he was showing me that his attire was no better than mine. His gesture and facial expression convinced me that he sincerely wanted me to come along. And, there was only one lady and there were three gentlemen which made the situation too out of balance, so I hesitatingly agreed to join them. Oh my, this is really getting wild, I thought, I have never done anything wild in my life before and I was truly ill at ease, but I could not let Wolfgang down. I was such a boring character. I finally decided, what the heck, Wolfgang would not enjoy the night without a dancing partner and for a change I should stop brooding over my heartaches. It was time to have fun!

I had not danced for years. Dance steps had changed; it was no longer as challenging as rock and roll. I was the best rock and roller in my teens. There were no more dance steps sequence to follow, and it had become all rhythmic body movements to go with the music. It is funny that they call this dance modern where to me it seemed that the primitive Africans had invented this way of dancing with body gyrations eons of years ago. It took me a little while to find my rhythm and body coordination for dancing and when I finally found it I danced away with Wolfgang in my house-slippers clad feet. I hoped nobody would look down on my feet. I tried to stay away from the dance lights and hoped that no one would recognize me. His business associates did not know what kind of woman I was. All they knew was that Wolfgang picked me up at the park. In the Philippines, strangers did not pick up reputable women so easily, so I was sure they were very suspicious of my character.

On our way back to Wolfgang's hotel from the nightclub, we passed by the Asian Development Bank- United Nations building complex and that was when I told them who I really was. I told them that I am a licensed Filipino Architect who was among the team that tackled the design of the ADB-UN building complex we were passing by. When it was time to say goodnight to everyone, I told them that I would take a taxi to go home. I did not want to be seen at my own neighborhood being taken home by strangers, that would have been a big scandal, which would surely start the gossipers' tongue wagging. I hailed for a taxicab. I had a fifty-peso bill in my purse. The taxi driver said he did not have change for my fifty, so the Filipino businessman lent me ten pesos in singles. I did not like that. I did not like it to appear that they paid me ten pesos for the night, but I did not want to give my fifty-peso bill to the taxi driver for a ten-peso fare so I accepted the offer.

Wolfgang had told me his departure time and date. I went to the airport to see him go and I gave him a hand carved wooden carabao as a memento. He said, "That's very gracious of you," when he accepted it. He had a very nice smile on his face, and he looked like he was touched by my gesture. I appreciated the brief encounter very much with Wolfgang who proved to be a most honorable gentleman. The attention he gave me was a salve to my wounded ego. He had given me so much comfort and had boosted my morale, which Junn had heartlessly trampled on. He had given me a beautiful little memory to cherish for a lifetime. Heaven knows that it was an honest innocent little encounter, which I needed so badly at the time. It made my problem with Junn more bearable. A recent movie entitled Lost in Translation reminded me of my encounter with Wolfgang because I thought they were very similar except my encounter was only for one evening.

Purely by chance, I came by the Filipino businessman who lent me ten pesos for the taxi fare at the lobby of an office building where I was informed Aida Cruz del Rosario was holding her office. I was very happy to give the businessman his ten pesos back which he accepted without hesitation. I came to the building to say hello to Aida for old time's sake and to satisfy my curiosity of why they decided to come back to Manila. I heard the sad story of what happened to the del Rosarios. When the Iligan Integrated Steel Mill was up and running they did not need the capable hands of Jose del Rosario anymore so the Jacintos who were the owners of the Steel Mill decided they could manage the company themselves, so they let Jose go. How typical, another story of how the rich exploits people for their selfish interests. It was not an easy task starting a steel mill going so they hired someone to do the hard job and when the operation began sailing smoothly, they did not need the man who did all the hard work anymore. I was sad to hear about how the Jacintos used the del Rosarios, but I was happy and relieved that

I was able to pay back the ten pesos that the businessman gave me for taxi fare.

I knew Apang was aware of what was going on in my married life. I remembered that at my wedding at the church, I glanced back and saw my Apang crying. I had never seen him cry before that. He was the only one who cried at my wedding. He admitted to me later on that he cried because for some reason he felt that my marriage to Junn would mean sufferings for me. Whatever he had feared on my wedding day had come true. When Holy Week was over, he came to see me and he told me, "You have been cooped up in your home too long. I believe working outside your home would be good for you. EARIST needs a Drafting Teacher, are you interested?"

Tentong was ready for preschool and my maids were all very trustworthy. My dress shop was operating smoothly with modest success, we had gained many regular customers some of them commissioned us for a custom-made dress weekly. I also found a master-cutter that my dress shop could operate without me. I accepted Apang's offer. EARIST evolved from my old Alma Mater RVHS, Rodriguez Vocational High School and it invoked precious memories of my happy high school days. It had evolved from a vocational high school to become Eulogio Amang Rodrigues Institute of Science and Technology where Apang worked as Property Custodian or Teasurer since the end of the Second World War.

I had to take courses in teaching because my degree in Architecture was not for teaching. EARIST offered the courses I needed. I was allowed to teach while I was taking the necessary teaching courses, such as Educational Psychology, Educational Sociology, and Methods of Teachings and Statistics.

Being a teacher took my focus away from my marital problems. Life had become more bearable. I enjoyed teaching and being with the students very much. At EARIST I spent my break times at Apang's office. The President of EARIST was the same Principal when I was still a student, Dr. Nudas. He and Apang had become like brothers. There was a new Vice President, Dr. Pada. He too became Apang's friend.

He oftentimes came to Apang's office to play chess with him at break time. One time he came but Apang was not there, so I played chess with him. That started a very good friendship between us. It was a friendship that developed into a great mutual admiration for each other. We had a beautiful platonic relationship. Men, I noticed, usually have a superiority complex over women. They do not like being outsmarted by a woman. Junn had once told me that he wished I would sometimes play dumb. Why should I pretend? I told him, why can't you appreciate me for what I am? Dr. Pada was someone who appreciated me for being me. I enjoyed very nice intellectual conversations with him. Unfortunately, there were some people who could not believe that a clean platonic relationship between a man and a woman was possible, but I did not have to worry about them as long as my conscience was clear. I answer only to a much higher Authority, God.

Working at EARIST gave me more time to spend with Apang. We had frequent lunches together. One of the places we went to for lunch sold hand crafted goods. A yellow, black and white batik print long dress hanging on a rack caught my attention. Apang bought the dress for me. To this day I treasure that dress and it will stay in my closet forever. I wear it occasionally. My size had not changed, and I intend to stay the way I am for the rest of my life.

On one of Apang's birthdays I sang the song "Oh My Papa" for him. I changed the last line from "I miss you so today" to "I love you so today" to make it more appropriate. I also changed Papa to Apang. He was so touched that he was crying. He asked me to sing that song to him on his birthday every year from then on and every time I sang the song for him, I saw tears rolling down his cheeks. Of course, this ended when I migrated to the US.

One day during summer break, I visited my college Alma Mater, Mapua Institute of Technology or MIT where I got my college education and training to become an Architect. I saw Oscar Benjamin Mapua, whom we call O.B. for short, which evolved into Obi, the grandchild of Tomas Mapua, the founder of the Institute. Obi was then the Dean of Architecture and Planning of the Institute. Obi and I, together with another student, George Trinidad and Nick Ricafrente who later on became the Dean of the School of Architecture and Planning of MIT, and an instructor Mr. Dee, whom we called Alo, sang together during my college years. We formed a quartet singing songs by Peter, Paul and Mary. MIT had a very sophisticated audio room for its time where we regularly practiced singing together and soon, we were performing during school programs. We even had a concert once to satisfy the students' requests. I remember that my older sister Mila attended this musical concert, and she said that some people in the audience said that we were only lipsing Peter, Paul and Mary records and I took it as a very nice compliment. Light travels faster than sound, people at the back seats of the concert saw our lips moving before they heard the sound, and we must really have sounded like Peter, Paul and Mary for them to think that we were merely lipsing. Obi. and I exchanged pleasantries at that meeting and when he found out that I was teaching at EARIST he said, "If you're teaching, why not here at MIT?"

Obi's offer was a very pleasant surprise for me, of course I would be very honored to teach Architecture. I declined accepting any more teaching assignments from EARIST and I started my new career as an Architectural Instructor at my own beloved Alma Mater MIT. The first semester was tough. I wanted to impart as much knowledge to my students the best way I could. I spent so much time on research to strengthen the contents of what I needed to teach, and I also started attending classes at the University of the Philippines for a master's degree in Architecture. I was assigned to teach Drawing to the freshmen, Color, Theory of Design, and History of Architecture to the upper classmen. It was a very challenging responsibility. For the freshmen, I adopted a program that gave them the chance to improve their drafting techniques and I allowed them to redo their plates if they were not satisfied with the marks they got, if they wanted to get a better mark. This arrangement meant more work for me, but I knew that the students appreciated the extra work I gave them because they presented me with a basket of flowers at the end of the semester, which was most gratifying. It was so gratifying as well to see all upper year Architectural students of my class fully attentive to my lectures. Students seated at the back whose view was obstructed by students in front of them leaned a bit to their sides so they could give me eye contact and to have caught their full interest meant to me that my deliberation of the subject matter was a success.

Meantime, when I became a MIT Faculty member, I noticed a change in Junn's demeanor, and I wondered if what I told him about Wolfgang made a difference. I did not know if he believed that nothing wrong had happened between this Italian businessman and myself and I don't think he did because he was the type who would never believe that a man and a woman can be in a hotel room together without sexual intimacy. I wondered if the possibility of a competition had brought back his proper senses. I noticed that he had been staying home more often. He also started a friendship with Rey, a very charming man, and his beautiful wife Via. This couple invited us to join their church, which was a born-again Christian Church. They convinced me to join the faith. I would do anything to save my marriage. Junn seemed attracted to the faith, so I joined in. I got dunked on the pool to be baptized to this new faith. Rey, Via, Junn and I became a constant foursome on weekends. Rey and Via had a very positive influence on Junn. The couple insisted whenever they invited Junn that my three children and I should come too. I was happy. My marital problems seemed to be over at last and I prayed that Junn would stay faithful forever.

Junn also started bringing home books written by an author named Ruth Montgomery. He said he wanted to know the truth. I was very hopeful that Junn would finally turn a new leaf and be a good father and husband who would spend some quality time with us. The year 1975 was very promising; I thought my troubles were over plus I just started an exciting career as MIT instructor. Ruth Montgomery's books fascinated me, and I read two of the three books that Junn had brought home.

Alas! Reading Ruth Montgomery's tales was exactly like opening Pandora's Box. What happened to me after reading Ruth Montgomery's books was allegorically like being swallowed by a dragon and she was the lure that led me to the mouth of the dragon. I was imprisoned in the dragon's belly for three months, but this dragon failed to digest me, and it was forced to vomit me out of its belly before I gave him a terrible indigestion. This terrible dragon released me, and I was back to my freedom on eve of the new year 1976. Five days later, while I was still pondering over the entire ordeal that I had just survived from, my mom surprised me with the flash of her camera to take my picture. This was the episode in my life that my mother wanted to keep secret and I know that she wanted to keep this story hushed up because no one can really explain what happened to me and some even thought that I have lost my sanity.

In the Philippines, having a relative with mental problems can cause a stigma to the entire family and I am the second of eight children. I have a dear cousin whose youngest brother had Downs syndrome. When her fiancé together with his parents, came to formally ask for her hand in marriage from my aunt and uncle, upon seeing her youngest brother with Downs syndrome, the mention of marriage was never brought out in the conversation and that was the end of the relationship of my dear cousin with her fiancé. She and her younger sisters never married. Only one sister who migrated to the U.S. was able to marry an American.

It was the two weeks semester break at MIT and I had so much free time so I wanted to know what truth Junn would find from Ruth Montgomery and so I read two of her books. Before I could start reading her third book, on October, 1975, I decided to do some experiment to test the allegations of Ruth Montgomery and that was when something very strange started to happen, something that turned out so horrible and yet enlightening. Today, as I look back in retrospect, I now know that it was a higher entity who was speaking to me revealing to me the truth, which at that time I could not comprehend and which I rejected because I perceived it as being contrary to my religious indoctrination. For the months of October, November and December of 1975, I fought against a force that was so vicious I ended up fighting for my life and for my sanity.

I am a witness to the existence of forces that modern science cannot yet detect. I know that there are others who had gone through this dimension who were less fortunate than me because I managed to get out unscathed, alive and sane, while the unfortunate others got imprisoned in this dimension permanently for the rest of their lives, their brains permanently damaged diagnosed as being schizophrenic. One big problem in our world is that most people in Academia are so arrogant and they believe they know it all and anything scientifically unproven in their accepted parameters are dismissed as hallucinations or imaginations gone wild and they give it the name – schizophrenia but they know nothing of what schizophrenia is all about. They do admit that they know nothing about it. They can identify the symptoms from the behavior of the afflicted, which they can observe but they cannot offer any explanation as to what causes it. I believe I found an explanation for this phenomenon, but I know that the scientific community will reject my explanation and the religious communities will find my explanation too radical or too unorthodox.

I remain hopeful that in time the explanation that I am trying to impart will be investigated by academia. In the past, some scientists who presented unorthodox ideas were scoffed at by the accepted scientific establishments, but further scrutiny proved their ideas to be correct like Faraday when he presented his idea of the presence of electro-magnetic energy, which was later backed by the mathematical calculations of James Clerk Maxwell. James Watson and Francis Krick believe that their discovery put an end to the debate: Does life have some magical, mystical essence? Is there something divine at the heart of a cell that brings it to life? They believe that the discovery of the double helix DNA answered that question with a definitive no. I disagree. I believe there are yet other energies that are still unknown to science that are vital components to life.

We burn calories when we think. The thought process converts calories to energy and thought energies do not just dissipate into nothing but is released by the human brain in the form of brain waves. The gathering of these brain waves is what I believe Dr. Carl Gustav Jung calls the collective unconscious and from it emanates specific collective brain waves with the same frequency, which can manifest. I believe that the energy that I encountered after reading Ruth Montgomery's books was a collective energy of brainwaves produced by people who nurtured destructive thoughts and religious superstitions. In the last three months of 1975, when all this weirdness was happening, I was not yet aware of the phenomenon of the collective unconscious, so I perceived the forces that were manifesting to me based on my religious indoctrination.

What I encountered was a kind of thought energy that tried to invade my thinking process, which somehow made me think that I was the one responsible for the malevolent thoughts that were entering my mind. Since I was fully aware that I never entertained evil thoughts, I vehemently rejected that I was responsible for evil suggestions that were trying to invade my mind. The experiment I conducted to put Ruth Montgomery's allegations to a test had caused my brain to be receptive to external collective brain waves, which happened to be an evil energy that was compelling me to murder people around me.

Because of my Christian upbringing I perceived the evil force as Satan. For the first time, I realized how indeed formidable the force of Satan is. It was very clear to me that Satan was trying to possess my thought process and I knew I had to fight him off at whatever cost. Science do not believe evil possessions, but I know it is true because I knew that at that time, the devil was doing everything in its power to possess me, to control my being, to do his vicious deeds and I knew I must stop Satan from using my body as his instrument of evil. This evil force was driving me to kill everyone around me. When Satan failed to turn me into a senseless mass killer, a nefarious energy took control of my hands that went to my neck to strangle me to death, which I later learned as what is called Alien Hand syndrome. I confronted this evil energy fearlessly, completely confident that evil will never triumph over good, and as soon as I focused on the saving grace of God, my hands were freed. Satan tried another means of killing me, several times, I experienced levitation while seated on a chair. As soon as I felt floating in air on my chair, I immediately dismounted before I was carried up high in the air and my chair would tilt so I would fall to my death. The fact that I survived the ordeal proved that my love for God and my devotion to the pursuit of goodness and righteousness was a guarantee of full protection from the power of Satan. I concede that it was my fault that I opened the door to let this evil entity into my life when I followed Ruth Montgomery's suggestion but on the other hand, I would never have come to the full understanding of what the force of Satan is if I did not experience its manifestation. Although Ruth Montgomery was the bait that led me to the jaws of the dragon, it was through my journey to the unknown that I found the truth. Today, paranormal manifestations believed to be ghost manifesting are on TV programs. I emailed the science channel that these ghost stories are propagating superstitious beliefs, but I was ignored.

While I was fighting against Satan's powers, I was seeing visions. I could not understand the meaning of the visions. Why were those visions shown to me? Before I experienced seeing visions, when I heard stories about people seeing visions, I did not know what seeing visions meant but when I started to see visions then I knew how it was. The images I saw were contrary to my Catholic indoctrination. At that time, I was a typical Catholic who had a small altar in my bedroom with the image of the crucified Christ hanging on my wall and a statuette of the image of Mary. Something was manifesting in both these religious articles, but they were in a manner that was tormenting me. The devil was telling me that these images were his agents too, so I asked my maid Marilyn to take them out of my room, burn them, bury them, just get rid of them, I wanted them out of my home and so everyone thought I was possessed by the devil. I knew that there was no one who could guide me and who could explain to me why those things were happening. I did not bother to see any religious authority about it because I knew they would be biased according to their beliefs. People around me were all convinced that I was possessed by the devil at that time. Father Robles, the Parish Priest at our Diocese who performed the wedding rites when Junn and I were married, was summoned to perform an exorcism rite for me but he declined. Why should I seek his advice? I was sure he would tell me that the visions were from Satan since they were contrary to Catholic beliefs.

The evil force that was manifesting to me had already convinced me that Satan is indeed alive and well but eventually, after fighting this evil force for three months, when my ordeal finally ended, and I was saved, I knew I did not do it alone. I knew that there is a Supreme Power above that delivered me to safety. I could not tell anyone what was truly happening at that time. I could not admit to anyone that there was a terrible force that was compelling me to murder everyone around me because I knew it would only confirm their suspicions that I was going insane. I was in full control of my mind, and I knew that there was nothing wrong with my sanity and my big dilemma was that no one would believe that I was fighting against an unseen diabolical force.

It would take another twenty-two years later on in my life, as I gained more knowledge of various forces that are created in our world with the guidance of a Supreme Power from Above that I came to a better understanding of what was causing the satanic force.

Every time I hear of a senseless crime, I get reminded of the evil satanic force that unsuccessfully compelled me to kill. Richard Speck committed his multiple murders of the poor innocent nurses where the only survivor and witness was Corazon Amurao, a Filipino nurse. What the evil force failed to make me do, Richard Speck did. This phenomenon made me understand why senseless murders get committed, why people kill for no valid reason at all. Why did I survive the ordeal and not succumbed to committing murder? Why are the others so easily manipulated by the evil force and turned them into vicious killers? Perhaps it is because my personality profile is different from them. Have I evolved out of the homo sapiens state in my life? In Houston, Texas, a woman named Andrea Yates killed all her five sons and no one can truly understand what made her commit such a heinous crime, but I do understand. I believe it is because she was subjected to this force much longer than I was and she ended up getting overpowered by this diabolical force after years of fighting against it. This diabolical force disguised as God, convinced Andrea that if she kills her children, they will be better off in heaven rather than grow up on this evil world. Satan is truly an effective sly operator on a quest to successfully annihilate all life on earth.

I made the conviction that I would never allow the dark sinister force to overcome me even if it meant taking my own life, which I knew would also be a triumph for Satan, but I thought killing myself would be a lesser evil than killing the innocent ones. The new semester had already started at MIT, and I had a new set of students attending the classes that were assigned to me but it came to a point where the ordeal made it impossible for me to concentrate on my lessons and I was becoming more concerned of the welfare of the students around me who would be endangered if I lose my war with Satan. I had no other choice but to stay away from my students at the University.

I lost my post as Instructor because of non-attendance. I did not know how to explain what was happening to me. What kind of explanation could I have given to Obi? My mother thought that I had a nervous breakdown caused by the stresses of my marital problem, but she was wrong because it happened at a time when my mind was at ease believing that my marital problem was over. I thought Junn's search for the truth meant following God's laws. My mother said, "Keep it hush-hush now that it is over. Get it out of your mind and get on with your life." My mother was right. At that time, I should get it out of my mind and just focus on my children and my new job at SSS. I remember that my maid Marilyn told me when I was back to my normal self, "Ate, I thought you have gone insane." I was not insane; I knew I encountered some forces that science has no means of detecting yet. I was so relieved when it was over that I was alive and sane. I was very grateful that all my maids, Marilyn, Naning, Virgie and Nara remained faithful to me during those three harrowing months of the terrible ordeal.

All my life I have pursued goodness and righteousness. I was a first grader at Pio del Pilar Elementary School when a young teen-age lady approached me and my playmates at the playground of RVHS one weekend and offered to give us catechism lessons. We all agreed, and this young lady devoted an hour of her life every Saturday, diligently teaching us the gospels of Jesus. She arranged our first communion when the time came that she believed we were all ready for this sacrament. That was how at an early age of six, I learned about Jesus, and I have accepted the philosophy of life that he recommended.

I was born with a natural artistic talent. I have been drawing pictures ever since I was a young child. I was the winner of an art competition for the whole city of Manila when I was a fifth grader at the Pio del Pilar Elementary School, and I was awarded the honor at the graduation ceremony of that school year. My entry to the art competition that won the award was a portrait of Elizabeth Taylor using crayons as my medium and I entitled it, My favorite Actress. When I told Mama that I wanted to be an artist, Mama said, "Pura, there are many starving artists, be an Architect instead." I thought artistic talent is also a necessary qualification to being a good Architect, so I agreed.

I was a fourteen year old high school student at RVHS on my third year, my nightmare those days was not being able to attend classes in school and I would not tell Mama when I was sick and in spite of having fever, I went to school. I paid badly for it. I began having severe back pains. Mama had me physically checked and the diagnosis was weak lungs, early stage of TB. My grandfather, Bernardino Cailao died of tuberculosis, and I was constantly exposed to him when I was an infant. I must have had the TB bug since then, but my strong immune system kept it at bay until I pushed myself to over exhaustion that empowered the TB bug to afflict me. I needed at least a month-long bedrest and a yearlong medication. I lost all chances for academic honors when I graduated from high school and the only award I got was being the best folk dancer of the year. It happened a second time on my second semester as a freshman at MIT, to take up a course in Architecture. I had to cancel my enrollment and the school gave me 50% of my tuition back since it was only the second week into the second semester. After a month bedrest, I felt healthy again, but my medication had to be taken a whole year. I had to wait for the next semester to get back to college, which was after another half a year. I should have graduated from college at age 21 but because of this ailment, I graduated from college at age 22. I had to get sick to continue the repeated pattern of 2 in my life.

At church I met Olive and invited me to join the Legion of Mary. I accepted and I made a devotion to the Lady of Lourdes. This started my daily church attendance. Every morning, I went to church to attend Mass dressed in white with a blue sash, the customary apparel of a Lady of Lourdes devotee, a practice that I later stopped when it started to make me feel that I was parading myself conspicuously for everyone to see how pious and pure I was, which to me was contradictory to my quest for humility following Jesus. The Legion of Mary devotees called each other sister. Sister Olive introduced to me a little book, The Imitation of Christ and from then on, this little book was my guide and source of great inner strength. I carried it with me in my purse everywhere I went. I read a passage each day from this little book while in a bus bound for school or wherever I was going to keep my mind from going astray to mundane thoughts and much more for protection from impure thoughts. I never entertained impure thoughts in my life.

Architectural subjects were offered only once a year at MIT and my pursuit to acquire a bachelor's degree in Architecture was delayed for a whole year. When I was healthy enough to enroll back at MIT, I met a new batch of classmates and one of them was Maloy. One time when we were alone at the ladies' room, I don't know what made her pull out a letter size portrait of a naked man in a grotesque posture of ecstasy with his genitalia in full erection and she showed it to me. I tried my best to hide from her how horrendously shocked I was to behold such an indecent image. I went to the privacy of the toilet stall and with my whole body shaken by the shock, I threw up. I prayed so hard to God and asked for forgiveness for allowing Maloy to expose me to such indecency. At eighteen years old, I was still so innocent of those facets of life. I was truly horrifyingly shocked. Was Maloy trying to indoctrinate me of earthly sexual pleasures, because I was so ignorant of it? I poured my attention to my academic pursuits and the Student Catholic Action organization. I was an active SCA cell leader and delegate to the SCA convention in Baguio.

When I was in my third year as an Architectural student, I started to work for a team of lady Architects Monette Alfaro and her partner Elena Bayot. I attended school evening sessions. It was then that I became exposed for the first time, what it meant to be an Architect. One must possess a very sociable personality to gain the clientele for a successful Architectural professional practice. I did not have any desire to be a social butterfly, that was just not me. I was content with my life devoted to spirituality as a Legion of Mary devotee. I told Mama that to be an Architect was not the kind of life I wanted. I told her that I really wanted a life dedicated to spirituality, I wanted to be a nun. Mama said, "Pura, you are my second child, you have six younger siblings, heaven forbid that something happens to your Apang, I might need your help to raise them." There could not have been a better response than what Mama said. Had she objected to my desire to be a nun for reasons that benefited me alone, I would have abandoned the path I was taking to be an Architect and went straight into the nunnery. What Mama said made me realize that I was being selfish, thinking only of what I want. She was correct, I must be at hand should help is needed for my siblings and I cannot do that as a nun. I entertained the attention of Junn to take my mind out of the nunnery.

CHAPTER 6

My Husband Said Goodbye

When I started working at the Philippine Social Security System, Junn started coming home late again but he had a very good excuse. He was enrolled at the University of the East for a master's degree. Every night around six he came home to shower and to change into a fresh outfit and then left again with the excuse that he was headed for the University. I had just come home from work one late afternoon when the phone rang. It was my mother; she was having a party and she wanted me to come right away. She was entertaining Jaime, a blonde, blue eyed American lady nurse who was visiting the Philippines. She was a friend and neighbor of my sister Anita in the US where she had become a resident since 1974. After meeting Jamie, I decided not to stay long at my mother's place after dinner because Jaime was busy talking to my other brothers and sisters anyway. I decided to go home to be with my children instead.

I came home while Junn was in the shower doing his usual after work freshening-up ritual. Except on choir rehearsal nights, I was usually home when Junn came to freshen up before he left for the University. That evening, my Maids told him that I was having dinner at my Mom's place. He was not aware that I was home, so a naughty idea sparked in my mind. I told my maids that I was going to spy on Junn and with my forefinger pressed over my tightly closed lips; I motioned to them not to tell. They all got thrilled with the idea, especially Virgie who was jumping up and down in her excitement. I tip-toed out of the apartment and sneaked into the back seat of Junn's car and slouched down low behind the driver seat so that he would not see my head from the rear-view mirror. I was still wearing my navy blue SSS office uniform because my mother's hasty invitation did not give me a chance to change into another outfit. I did not have my purse with me but I had some money on my pocket. If Junn would see me, I would get out of the car, maybe give him an impish smile for getting caught, end of the story.

All my maids were watching from the window when Junn hastily got in the car. He did not see me at all because he was too busy looking to his left and to his right, probably checking if I was anywhere in sight, unsuspecting that I was inside the car. Also, the navy blue SSS uniform dress I was wearing must have made me the more inconspicuous. Virgie told me later that they were all cheering when Junn drove away not knowing that he had me as a passenger behind him. From where I was, slouched back as low as I could, all I could see was the skyline of the buildings alongside the road, but I recognized the silhouette of Santo Domingo Church against the dimming sky as we passed by and I was assured that the route we were taking was indeed the way to the University of the East. I started planning my next move. I envisioned myself secretly getting out of the car at the parking lot, after he had left, and taking a bus home.

I had never done any spying at all in my life, and I was so nervous. I discovered that when you are scared your mouth dries up. My upper lip got stuck to my upper front teeth because of dehydration; I had to unstick it with my tongue. I buried my hands on each of the big side pockets of my dress to keep them from shaking. On one pocket I held some loose coins securely on my one hand to prevent them from making jingling sounds while the car was moving. On my other pocket I nervously held my office I.D.

Before we got to the University, we suddenly turned left to a residential section of Manila. The pounding of my heart got heavier. Oh, no, I thought, am I going to discover something illicit? Oh, calm down Pura, don't be too dirty minded, he is just picking up a classmate, I tried to assure myself. We stopped in front of an apartment building. Junn got out and took some books with him. See Pura, he is going to study some lessons with a classmate, I kept assuring myself.

I pulled myself up from my slouched position to see where he was going. I watched him walk toward an apartment door. A woman greeted him (thank God it was not Remy). But then she gently caressed his back, then both of them disappeared from my view. Oh no, I did not like what I saw. I was deeply perturbed so I got out of the car. There were some teenagers hanging out on the roadside and they all gave me a very curious look when they saw me emerge from the back seat of the car. "Huli!" one of them said, which means caught you! I ignored the onlookers and went as close as I could to the door where they had disappeared. My knees were shaking; I was afraid discovering something ominous would be the outcome of my spying. I sat on a knee-high concrete plant box next to the entrance door because my knees could no longer hold me erect from too much shaking. I was hoping that I could hear their conversation to get a clue to what their meeting was about. I was still holding on to the thought that they were classmates preparing for their lessons. I did not want to embarrass myself barging in an innocent study session. I could not hear anything, so I mustered all my courage and stood up. I slowly walked towards the door, which they had left open, a very common practice in the Philippines because homes are not airconditioned. I saw Junn with this woman in a romantically jovial tête-à-tête, which was immediately interrupted by my sudden appearance. I could not say a word. Junn was startled and completely flabbergasted by my unexpected appearance and his startled look quickly turned into a dreadful venomous stare. I looked at him with a big hurt and a big why painted all over my face while his eyes glared at me in a way that made me understood what comic drawings of daggers coming out of irate eyes meant because his eyes looked that way. The woman spoke first; she must have seen the way Junn and I were staring at each other. She broke the icy silence," I don't understand," she said.

My hands were still in my dress pockets and my right hand was still holding my SSS identification card. I handed her my I.D. and I finally found my voice, "I am his wife, and we have three children. Here is my I.D" and I handed her my ID.

She took my I.D., looked at it then raised her hand to her forehead and closed her eyes and her face grimaced in disbelief. She was apparently another victim of Junn's deception. She handed me back my I.D. I felt sorry for her; I could see she was deeply hurt.

Junn came to me, grabbed my arm and dragged me out of the apartment saying, "Let's get out of here". He pushed me towards the car. "How did you find me?" He furiously asked fuming mad.

"I followed you in a taxicab," was my first reply. I can never be a good liar. I made the mistake of adding, "Virgie helped me get the cab."

"Virgie is fired!" He thundered.

"Don't fire Virgie, you brought me here. I was at the back seat of your car!" I admitted.

"Why did you have to hurt her? Why did you have to show yourself, why didn't you wait till I got home to tell me!" He was screaming at me like a maniac.

"Hey, what's happening here. Has the world turned upside down? I'm the one who's supposed to be screaming at you. All your concern is for her. What about my feelings? Don't you think I was hurt more than her?"

Junn continued his irrational tongue lashing at me, he angrily repeated, "Why did you have to show yourself to her?"

He had completely gone mad.

"You did not want her to see me so you can continue your masquerade, so you can continue deceiving her! That's what you want, isn't it?" I was completely aghast. He did not show any concern for me at all. He was a very different man from the apologetic husband who asked for forgiveness for having an affair with Remy.

My older sister Mila and her husband Mo were at our apartment when we got home. My Mom's party was over, and they stopped by to say hello because I left them before we could say any greetings to each other. My maids told them about my spying stint. When the door opened and Junn and I appeared, they knew something awful happened as soon as they saw the unspoken indignations in our countenance. Our body language conveyed to them that their presence was inappropriate, and they made an immediate exit quietly. I heard Mo say sometime later," If I did not see what happened with my own eyes, I would have said, those kinds of stories only happen in the movies, not in real life; only in the movies" Well, it happened for real to me, Ms. Adversity.

I got a surprise call from Junn's woman at the office the following day. Apparently, the information on my office ID was very easy to remember, RED SSS, so she knew exactly how to reach me. She wanted to meet me at a restaurant to talk. I agreed. Her name was Yolanda, Yoly for short. Just like Remy, I had no reason to be hostile to Yoly. She was another victim of my pretentious philandering husband. I told her that Junn had a history of womanizing.

"Don't worry about me, I am not a home wrecker. I'll stay away from him," she promised. I prayed that she would keep her word.

Junn made no effort to console me. He had no qualms in openly expressing his opinion on the necessity of having a divorce in the Philippines. He acted like the forlorn lover who was inconsolably heartbroken. To him I was the cruel witch who had him trapped. I learned later on that he relentlessly stalked Yoly until she gave in. Their affair resumed with invigorated fervor.

Yayoy's rendition of Chopin's nocturne became more meaningful to Junn because of Eddie Dutchin's modern adaptation that made it into a song with the lyrics, "No heart should refuse love. How lucky are the ones who choose love and if we should lose love, we have the right to love again."

He asked Yayoy to play the piece almost every morning until Yolanda accepted him again. The change in his demeanor was very apparent. Although he never admitted to anything, I knew what was going on and it hurt terribly.

One early evening Yayoy and I were on our way home from the Cubao shopping malls after a shopping spree when a traffic light held up our bus at EDSA. Guess who was right next to us? Yayoy immediately recognized his father's car. I looked down from the bus window to see Yolanda on the passenger's seat. Yayoy, at the tender age of seven told me, "Mama, we did not see anything, alright. We did not see anything." He knew that what he had seen meant a quarrel between his father and me again and he dreaded to see us quarrelling. I know that I had been bad too for not controlling my emotions in front of the children, but I was hurting so badly.

What does a woman do in this desperate situation in a country where the law did not allow divorce? What does a woman do when her husband openly shows her that his love had died? He blatantly told me that he could not live without her. I tried to take my mind away from the tormenting situation as much as I can. At work I accepted all the out-of-town assignments. I volunteered to take all the away assignments to the different Islands of the Philippines. I made trips with my different Supervisors to the different provinces. I was with Atty. Baybay, the chief of our section, on the Island of Palawan to inspect the ongoing construction of a hospital. SSS granted loans for the construction of hospitals as well.

I was with Mars Foronda, the Chief of the Credit Division of our Department on a mission to Malaybalay, Cotabato, a province in the island of Mindanao to investigate the feasibility of a loan application. On the plane, I came by Eddie, the valedictorian of our class at RVHS. It was nice to see him again. The seat next to him was vacant and he asked me to sit next to him. I was such a stupid strict complier to rules, and it would be so uncomfortable for me to take a seat not assigned for me because I would always be worried that I would be sent away when the rightful seat occupier came along. I was not on a pleasure trip. I was being paid by the System for the trip. I thought that Mars, who was my Superior on that business trip, might discuss our itinerary with me so I declined Eddie's invitation. I also was not ready to announce my failing marriage to anyone. I saw Eddie's demeanor abruptly changed. He might have thought I was doing something illicit with my Superior. I tried to catch him on our way out, but he made it obvious that he did not want to talk to me. I was thinking, "Oh Eddie, it is not what you think."

Christmas was drawing near. I kept asking Junn to go shopping with me for the children. I was still hoping that he would have a change of heart and abide with Philippine laws that forbid divorce. But he was determined to make my life miserable. Aside from coming home at dawn, his weekends were devoted to Yolanda. He was also becoming reckless with his finances. Two men from the bank came to repossess his car. He must have been spending his money for Yolanda instead of making car payments. Did Yolanda give in to his wooing and broke her promise to me because he had been showering her with gifts? Shamelessly, he asked me to borrow money from Mama and Apang so that he can keep his car. I wanted to save my marriage for my children's sake. I called Mama. Mama and Apang were also doing everything they can to save my marriage. They did not hesitate to help. Mama immediately came with the cash needed to prevent the bank from repossessing his car.

On the weekend before Christmas, I insisted that we were going shopping for the children. It was the last chance we had to go shopping for the children's Christmas presents. I held on to his arms and I told him that I was not letting him go anywhere except to do some shopping with me for the children. He forcibly freed himself and as he did so, my fingernail accidentally caused a little abrasion on his lip, which bled a little bit. He touched his lip where he felt the sting and when he saw the tiny bit of blood on his finger he erupted into a rage. He twisted my arm violently. I was fortunate to be limber enough to turn my body while he twisted my arm to prevent my arm bone from coming off its socket. He pushed me and I fell on the steps of the stairs that led to the second floor of our apartment. His pair of shoes was on one of the steps. I grabbed one shoe and hurled it at him. He caught it and hit me with it over and over everywhere in my body like a devil-possessed maniac in full rage.

His frenzy of madness went on and on and I thought he would not stop until I was dead. He kept hitting me everywhere. I was down on the floor, and I could not get up because his blows kept coming. I heard all my three children's terrified cries. I was helpless, all my maids were too scared to interfere and there was nothing I could do to avoid his blows while I was worrying that my children were witnessing their father's violent insanity.

When he decided to stop whacking me, perhaps his arms got too exhausted, I immediately got to my feet and took my three crying terrified little ones into my arms, and I tried to console them as much as I could. When everything calmed down, all I could say to Junn was, "This is what I got for taking care of you at the hospital." I have never said anything about the hospital care I gave him before that. It was the first time I ever mentioned it.

His reply was a scornful, "Are you God?"

We all went shopping for the children after all the unfortunate agitation died down. I walked with them at the mall feeling like a zombie. I was too shocked, too numbed to feel the pain. My thoughts were on my children. I had to do the shopping for my children. What did Yolanda do to my husband. What kind of power did she possess that changed my husband into a cruel heartless beast?

I went to work the following Monday black, blue, green and purple. I could not hide my bruises because my entire body was bruised. I had to wear the mandatory uniform to work, which was the navy-blue knee length dress with short sleeves. Atty. Baybay was so concerned. He sent me to the infirmary on the ground floor of the SSS building to be checked. I did not have any broken bone, thank God, but my bruises did not go away for almost a month.

I was on counter duty three weeks after Christmas. While attending to a horde of loan applicants, I saw Mama suddenly appear on the main entrance doorway to our department. She quietly sat at a vacant seat at the waiting area and patiently waited until I was done attending to a loan applicant. I knew why she came. Before I could call the next applicant, she sat on the chair where applicants sat by me on the opposite side of the counter. "Why didn't you tell us?" She asked deeply concerned and almost in tears. I knew my maids had told her.

"What good would it do, Ma? There was really nothing you could have done." There was really nothing I could say to my mother. She left. I could tell how very sorry she was for me.

That Christmas of 1977 was the saddest Christmas ever for me. Junn was not with us. He stayed with her, but he kept denying that he was still seeing her. I wanted to end my agony but what can I do?

January 28, 1978, I went to the same apartment where I first met Yolanda. She was not home. I found out that she was renting a room from a landlady. The landlady asked who I was. I told her the truth. She was very understanding, and she openly showed her sympathy for me. In a country where there is no divorce, all wives sympathize with the wife of a philandering husband. She allowed me to wait for the couple to arrive. Yolanda and Junn arrived right after my conversation with the Landlady. Yolanda immediately went into a childish frenzy as soon as she saw me, "Siya eh! Siya eh! "(It's his fault! It's his fault!)" she frantically said while pointing to Junn acting like a silly little child who was caught stealing a cookie from the cookie jar. Once again, I did not say a thing. I just wanted Junn to know that he could not deny anymore that their affair was still going on. I started to walk towards the door to leave but Junn grabbed me by the sleeve of my jumpsuit and dragged me out of the apartment. Fortunately, my jumpsuit, which I had sewn myself, was of a very strong khaki fabric. It did not come apart when Junn viciously jerked me. I staggered and almost fell but being an agile athlete, I kept my balance when he wickedly jerked me in front of the two women. He was determined to embarrass me in front of Yolanda and her landlady.

When Junn and I were already in the car, I noticed that Yolanda followed and wanted to get in the car. It was a two-door car and the only way she could get in was for me to unlatch my backrest forward to give her room to get into the back seat. I did not know where my emotion was at that time; my compassion once again took over. I leaned forward and let her in. I was small enough to be able to give her enough room to get in the back seat of the car without me getting off. I was caught in this love triangle. Junn and Yolanda's lust for one another was unstoppable and I was a hindrance for them. Junn did not love me anymore; I should just let him go but our laws would not let me. What about my children, they have all the right to have the love and care of their father? I had to fight for what was right for my children.

Junn took us to a Kentucky Fried Chicken restaurant. We got seated on the first empty booth that we could find. After a few quite awkward minutes I decided to break the silence to get it over with as soon as possible and with a very calm voice I said to Junn looking at him straight in his eyes, "Now you have to make your decision, is it her or us?" I was still hoping that Junn would choose to obey the law and stay with my children and me.

"I'm moving out, I'm packing up," he coldly replied. It was the ultimate insult of my life. He dumped me right in front of the other woman. I took the indignity civilly.

"Very well, you have to give me the car keys." I calmly said.

"That car is not yours," he retorted.

"It is not yours either until you pay my Mama and Apang their money." I was sure that Yolanda did not know that he would have almost lost his car if my parents did not lend him the money to save his car from being repossessed by the bank.

He got up, took the key out of his pockets and banged it on the table towards me. I took the key and quietly got up and started towards the door. I was in a daze. My marriage was over, so what, it had been hell from the beginning anyway. I should really celebrate because I had been freed from hell, yet I could not celebrate. My children only see their father while he is still in bed in the morning before they go to school but at least they see him everyday. Now that he had decided to move out my children would not see him anymore. What have I done; I drove my children's father away? No, I did not drive him away; I gave him an excuse to leave.

I had a driver's license, but I never really dared drive in the crazy Manila traffic. I guess I have to dare drive this time; oh, I was too numbed to think. When I got to the car, I found both of their jackets on the seats. *Forgive, turn your other cheek*, yes, I have to turn my other cheek. I gathered the two jackets, what would I do with them, throw them out on the road, can I really do that? I have never done anything mean in my life; I did not know how to be mean. But they deserve it, they don't deserve my kindness. No, I can never be mean. I started walking back to the restaurant to give them their jackets. *Love thy enemy*, my little book said love thy enemy. I carried the jackets back to the restaurant.

When I got back to them, I saw Junn lovingly comforting the tearful Yolanda. Why was she crying, she triumphed over me, was it tears of joy? They deserved each other. I cannot feel sorry for Yolanda anymore. She was no longer a victim this time. She was a co-conspirator. She promised she would not break my home, what a liar. Junn knew I could not drive. He told Yoly to wait for him at the restaurant and he walked with me back to the car. He drove me home in complete silence.

Junn was busy packing his clothes as soon as we got home. My poor children, how will they grow up without a father? I had heard of broken homes producing wayward children. My whole being was suddenly engulfed by the dreadful fear of not knowing how my children would grow up in a broken home. What have I done, oh what have I done? I could no longer contain myself, I started to cry, I pleaded to him, "Please stay for the children's sake. You don't have to be my husband, just be a father to my children. You don't have to sleep with me. I'll make the study your bedroom, I beg you, please stay!"

He did not say a word. His heart had turned to stone. He left us to be with Yolanda. His lust for this woman had overcome his reason. How did I end up with a man who cared only for his own selfish desires? How can he father three innocent lives in this world and carelessly abandon them at their tender age unconcerned of how they would fare in this cruel world? How can one live peacefully within himself with this kind of guilt, or does he have any feeling of guilt at all? How could I have known that this was how he would turn out to be? No, I cannot have regrets; I love my three children too much to have regrets.

It was so strange; I dreamt that I was Catherine of Aragon, the first wife of Henry the eighth. The dream was so real; I even remember how uncomfortable it was to be wearing the heavy voluminous gown that was so tight on my chest and how laborious it was to move about in the heavy queenly garb. Was my dream making an analogy between Catherine and myself? Junn was behaving exactly like Henry the eighth. Catherine died of a broken heart. No, I could not die because of this; I have three children to look after. I must survive.

The emotional trauma started to cause havoc in my physical being. I had lost my appetite to eat but I had to fight to survive. I prayed with every spoonful of food that I put in my mouth to reach my belly because my system seemed to reject any kind of nourishment. Every time the thought of Yolanda and Junn came to my mind, I could feel the vile that my stomach excreted, and I started having stomach pains. I remembered an article I have read about how people can burn your energy without them even knowing it. I suddenly understood what it meant. I cannot let them burn me. I decided that I should conduct an experiment and make a guinea pig of myself. The reason that I was so much in pain was that I was so indignant at the way my husband had treated me. My ego was hurt. If I take away my ego, if there will be no more me, then there is no one to hurt, then I can take any punishment and I shall not be hurt any more. "Cast thy burden on the Lord," that was one of the songs I sing in church, from now on I would cast all emotional burden to the Almighty Higher Being so I would be free of any emotional pain. But my concern and worry for my children was overwhelming. What concerned my being, I could control but the fear of the ominous threat of the situation to my children was something I could not control. I could not focus on my work. I asked Attorney Baybay to allow me to go on a sick leave for a month. I had worked with the System long enough that I have earned a month sick leave with pay. Atty. Baybay was very understanding.

Three weeks after my leave I stopped by at the office after I picked up my paycheck. Atty. Baybay noticed how skinny I had become, and he told me that the vacation was not doing me any good. He suggested that it would be better therapy for me to report back to work. I agreed with him, and I resumed my duties after a three-week leave. I was only eighty-nine pounds when I had my physical check up before working again. I had lost sixteen pounds.

Days passed. The children started to notice that their father had not come home. Yayoy asked, "Mama, where is Papa, I haven't seen him for days?"

"He is on vacation somewhere, Yayoy," was my excuse. I could not tell him that his father decided to live with someone else and I was still hoping that Junn would realize that he made a mistake and would come back to my children. Raqui and Tentong were too young to be affected by the situation. They were too engrossed with their toys but Yayoy was devastated. He felt his father's rejection as much as I did.

After several weeks, Junn came to visit. Yayoy asked him, "Papa, why aren't you coming home anymore?

"I'm here right now. I'm here to see you,"

"Yes, but you are just visiting, you don't live with us anymore." Yayoy's words were crushing my heart. My poor son was hurting too. His precocious mind knew a family is not complete without a father. He was just as crushed as I was when his father left again.

I spent more time with the children at night. I thought them to play old maid with the playing cards. The queen of cloves was left out of the game and the cards were paired with another similar card in color and in number. At the end of the game the holder of the queen of spade was the old maid. The old maid wore a silly hat as punishment until the next old maid was found. They all had a kick when I was the old maid wearing the silly hat.

When they got bored playing old maid, I taught them to play hearts with the deck of cards. They enjoyed the games so much. Tentong was only five years old, and his little fingers could hardly hold all the thirteen cards in one hand, but he could play the game, which required mental agility. When we were not playing cards, we went to the Parks and Wildlife with all the maids. There were nights when we took our supper to the park and had picnics. Once in a while we went to Luneta Park for a change. I kept the children occupied and entertained to keep their minds from wondering again where their father was.

My Auntie Gene, the husband of Uncle Epeng, the parents of my cousin Ding who gave me the hint about Junn's continued philandering, who were our neighbor, had lunch with us one day. We were seated around the dining table when suddenly Yayoy got up and ran towards the door of my dress shop. I heard the door bang and then I saw him ran back to his seat. I could not see the door from where I was seated but Auntie Gene could. The door had one big glass pane so the person on the other side can be seen. "Oh dear, Yayoy banged the door to his Papa's face," I heard my aunt say, her voice sounded very concerned. It was the first time I saw Yayoy express his anger towards his father. It had been over a month since his father came for a visit and he must have thought that if his father couldn't live with us, he might as well stay away. He must have been really hurt that he didn't want to see the person hurting him anymore.

"Yayoy, the Law said, honor thy father and thy mother. He is your father, open that door," I said to my eight year old son with authority.

"Mama, I wish you did not marry Papa."

"Yayoy, if I did not marry your Papa and I married someone else, I would have a son, but it would not be you. You are you because of your father's genes and mine. Go open that door."

Yayoy reluctantly obeyed. He went back to the door to let his father in. We did not know what the purpose of his visit was. We really had nothing to say to each other. He had nothing to say to Yayoy either. Perhaps the presence of my auntie Gene made it hard for him to say anything so he just hang out for a bit, took a seat at the couch in the living room and then left. After his father had left, Yayoy told me, "I will never marry."

"Tell me that again when you are fifteen." I told him.

"What if my wife leaves me too?" Yayoy worriedly asked.

"It doesn't happen to everyone, Yayoy. Because it happened to me doesn't mean that it will happen to you too," was my reassuring reply. Yayoy is fifty four now and he is still a confirmed bachelor.

Yayoy was definitely devastated by his father's leaving. He suffered the rejection as much as I did. Tearfully and in a sobbing voice he asked me, "Mama, what can we do so that Papa would come home?" I made a big mistake of saying, "Maybe we should pray and ask God to send your Papa home." Being Catholics the only prayers that we knew was to say the rosary so Yayoy said, "Let's say the Rosary so Papa would come home." In spite of my horrendous ordeal with my rosary, I couldn't reject Yayoy's request, as Catholics, it's the only way of praying we knew. Every night we prayed, I led the prayer and Yayoy, Raqui and Tentong joined me in the Lord's prayer, the Hail Mary and the Glory be. Night after night Yayoy would remind us to start our rosary but his Papa never came home. This suggestion to ask God to send his father home would haunt me later. Yayoy also stopped playing Chopin's Nocturne. In fact, to this day, he would make all kinds of excuses not to play this peace, which he used to love to play for his father when he was a child. I don't even think that he still remembers why he can't play this music again, but it is probably buried deep in his sub-conscious.

One day, while Yayoy was still going through the trauma of losing his father (to another woman), I received a note from Claret school. The note said that he was not paying attention inside the classroom. Oh no! Not my smart Yayoy. I immediately went to see his teacher to see what was wrong. His teacher told me that all day long Yayoy would stare out of the window and not pay attention to the lessons.

I pleaded with the teacher to give Yayoy some understanding, and I was forced to tell her about the situation at home. Somehow, Yayoy overcame the trauma. He satisfied all the school requirements at the end of the school year to qualify for promotion to the next level. In fact, every year after that he brought home a gold medal for being the best in science. He had successfully led his team representing their school to become the champion of a televised student competition in Manila before he graduated from Claret School.

I did not want my children to harbor any negative feeling to anyone much more towards their father. I tried to make them understand that they have to understand their father too. When Yayoy asked, "Mama, why is Papa like that?"

"Maybe Mamang did not teach him good enough. That is why you have to learn from this. You should know that you should never forsake your own children when the time comes," I told him.

I knew that one way to relieve the anguish in my heart was to learn to accept that Junn would not be with me anymore and I was willing to do that because all he had given me were miseries anyway but to accept that my children would grow up without a father was harder to accept. With all the stories about wayward children being the product of a broken home that I heard about, I was so fearful of how my children would grow up, but I did not know what else to do. I tried to stop thinking about this mishap that happened to my marriage, there was nothing to gain dwelling on it. I tried to focus my thoughts on other things.

I diverted my attention to a piece of real estate property. I thought that someday I would be able to build my home on it, just for my children and me. I wanted to buy it, but it was not fair to share it with Junn because he was already living with Yolanda. According to our law anything I bought was conjugal because I was married. I thought of Sylvia Atencia, one of my classmates at the University of the Philippines where I attended a master's degree course in Architecture. She became a very good friend of mine. Her father was a lawyer, Atty. Atencia. She arranged for me to meet with him. He advised me that I should get a legal separation. If I were legally separated, I could buy any property and be the sole owner.

Atty. Atencia told me what documents to prepare to obtain a legal separation. The only way I could comply to the requirements was to know where Junn and Yolanda were residing. My old spying stunt came back to my mind. I pulled it once; I can pull it again. Junn never again left his car door unlocked after I had successfully pulled that spying stunt. However, he had kept a spare key for his car in the drawer at the study which I believe he had already forgotten. I accidentally found it when I was looking for something. So, one night when he visited the children, I made the excuse that I was going to see my mom. I was wearing blue jeans and a dark shirt. I secretly slipped into his car back seat once again, this time I sat on the floor behind the passenger seat. I was tiny, I could fit anywhere. I quietly waited and just like before, he unsuspectingly drove away. He took me to where he resided. I successfully pulled my spying stunt for the second time. He did not suspect that I would pull that same trick twice. Well, he was wrong.

It was dark of night. I waited for a few seconds after I heard the door slam shut before I peeked. I watched him walk towards an apartment building and waited until he was inside his unit before I got off the car. I took a taxi home, and I went back the following day. This was Junn and Yolanda's first home. I knocked and their maid Naty opened the door. She was the same maid Yolanda had when I discovered them, and she recognized me. She let me in. The maid must have been aware of our law, and she must have known that her masters were lawbreakers because she did not prevent me from taking the evidence that Atty. Atencia asked me to gather. I found a picture of Junn and Yolanda together, his arm was around her shoulder. It was very strong evidence because it proved that they knew each other.

Their two lady neighbors, Violeta Bulante and Lourdes Velasquez, were both very sympathetic to me. All Filipino wives are sympathetic to a wronged wife, in fact one of them was so kind to tell me, "I don't know what he saw in her because you are prettier than her." They both signed notarized affidavits that Yolanda and Junn presented themselves as man and wife. They both agreed to testify in court for me. I had all the evidence needed to get my legal separation. Junn and Yolanda must have moved to a new home after learning from their maid about my visit.

One of the loan applicants at SSS was the secretary of a Judge in Quezon City. I mentioned to her my plan of obtaining a legal separation. She apparently knew that obtaining a legal separation was not as simple as I thought. She arranged an appointment for me to see the Judge for advice. I brought all my documents and showed them to the Judge. The Judge told me that to get a legal separation, I had to prove that my husband was guilty of concubinage, which was punishable with imprisonment according to our laws. Once I file my case in court, my evidence will become state evidence and the state will have to prosecute. I would not have the option to withdraw because it is a criminal offence. The evidence I had gathered was enough to send Junn and Yolanda to prison. That was how tough it was when the law did not allow divorce.

The Judge told me to consider the consequences of the matter with regards to my children. Other children would ostracize them if it became known that their father was in prison. He said, "My policy in life is live and let live." He was a liberal Judge.

Atty. Atencia did not inform me of the severity of the case. I had no intentions of sending Junn to jail. Atty. Atencia, who was a nemesis of womanizers, was furious when I backed out. He said, "In the future if you change your mind, find yourself another lawyer." I bought the real estate property in my father's name.

Before Yolanda got deeply involved with Junn I tried everything I could do to stop their unlawful relationship. I wanted my children's father to come home. Her landlady gave me an address of her relatives. My next-door neighbor was so sympathetic and so kind to offer to give me a ride and help me locate Yolanda's relatives. I did not hesitate to inform them that Yolanda was having an affair with my husband with the hope that they would be instrumental in ending this relationship, which is unaccepted in Filipino norm of morality. It soon became apparent that none of Yolanda's relatives could make her change her mind. I pleaded with them to keep trying but when her uncle told me, "Yoly must be better than you in bed that's why your husband left you for her," I knew I should not call them again ever. I could not allow myself to be insulted further by people who have lower moral standards. However, a few months later, they were the ones who called me and asked me to help them locate Yolanda because she had disappeared.

Junn had become the manager of an oil distribution company when a pretty married woman named Vilma started working with him. They had become good friends instantly. Vilma invited Junn to join her family and friends to a picnic in a lake somewhere in Laguna and she insisted that Junn's wife, not the mistress, should be with him. That was how I came to know Vilma. The picnic was in a beautiful scenic lake that looked to me like it was created by an impact of a huge meteor. It looked like a smaller version of the Meteor Crater in Arizona, which got filled up with water. They said that the lake is very deep, and I was wondering if the meteorite was still at the bottom because it looked like it landed on soft soil, which formed the crater walls after the impact. Vilma was very amiable to me and she expressed her sympathy and she told me that she would help me get my husband back. She told me that she had been persuading Junn to go back home to us where he should rightfully be. She was so sweet and righteous, and we became immediate friends.

When Yolanda's relatives called me to help them locate their missing daughter, I called Vilma hoping that she could tell me where Junn and Yolanda were residing because they had moved out of the previous address which I have located after my second detective work. Perhaps they did not feel comfortable because of the fact that I knew where they lived. Perhaps they worried that I would harass them which was silly because I will never lower myself to their level. Vilma did not know the exact address, but she knew the general vicinity. She came up with the plan of asking Junn to give her a ride to a specific location and that I should be there in a taxicab waiting at the exact time we agreed on, ready to follow Junn on his way home. The plan worked very well. I was in a taxicab at the exact time Vilma told me she would be dropped off by Junn and I told the taxicab driver to follow Junn's red car wherever it went. Upon learning where they were residing, I gave the information back to Yolanda's relatives. Vilma told me that Yolanda did not disappear; she was hiding from her relatives because she was pregnant.

Several months later, my inspection site happened to be in the neighborhood where Junn and Yolanda were residing. My SSS driver Brigitte was driving me around in the SSS land rover. I estimated that Yolanda's baby would be born by then and I thought I would like to come see the half brother of my children. Their maid was still Naty, the same made Yolanda had from the first time I discovered the affair, and she did not hesitate to let me in the apartment. She knew I was the wife of Junn. I saw a little baby boy in a crib, and I picked him up and gently rocked him in my arms. I told the little two months old baby, "I have nothing against you. It was not your fault." I did not stay long; I had more inspection sites to visit.

Whatever Junn had done to me, I could never stop caring for him anymore. My love for him transcends that passionate love a woman feels for a man. Ever since I took care of him in the hospital, he had taken a permanent spot in my heart; he had become one of my sons. Just like a little boy who needed care and understanding. A little boy trapped in a grown man's body forever. What had caused such a tragedy? What had caused such insecurity that he needed the attention of these lustful women to give some semblance of worthiness to his meaningless existence? It seemed that when responsibilities start creeping in the relationship he was having with a woman, his lust ebbs, and his quest for a new conquest gets invigorated. It must be his insecurity that made him start a new relationship without breaking the previous one first. He wanted to be assured that there would always be someone at hand in case his new conquest fails. What motivates men like Junn to go on this unending cycle of quest for a new lustful relationship and go on to a new one when the lust dies? Don't they ever feel any guilt? Once again, the purpose of life is to be happy. Was Junn going on this vicious cycle of conquests and escapades because he believed it will bring him happiness? He apparently did not care that he was hurting all these women he had left behind. All he cared for was the satisfaction of his sexual desires. What a selfish man he truly was. He did not care for the welfare of the children at all. He did not give any financial support for my children when he left.

He called me at work one time asking for two hundred pesos. I said, "What is this Junn, when you have money, you are with your women and when you need money, you think of me?"

"Are you giving me money or not?" He shamelessly retorted.

"Well, come over." I conceded.

Edna, who had become a close friend and a confidant, was within hearing distance asked, "What was that all about?" I told her what it was about.

"If I have a hammer, I'm going to hit you on your head to make you come to your senses," She said.

I was in full control of my senses. I was trying to buy Junn back so that my children would have a father again. Junn demanded more money from my parents for his old car. My parents, who were doing everything they can to patch my marriage agreed. My brother Oyet needed a car anyway. Junn blatantly told me that for my parents he wanted the full amount but if his fraternity brother would buy his car, he was willing to give it for two thousand pesos less and he said it scornfully. Why did he have to say that to me? What was he punishing me for? I really did nothing wrong to him to deserve his punishments. Sure, I made him know how I felt about his selfishness, all he cared for was his own selfish desires and he never cared about the consequences of his actions toward our children, but it was always in a normal tone of voice and never screaming, I am not a screamer. He had really turned so evil. What could Yolanda have done to convert what used to be a nice caring person into a monster. It seemed that the devil that tried to possess me possessed Junn instead to torment me but he could not hurt me anymore, I was beyond that. When I decided to follow the prayer of one of the Saints who was a follower of Jesus, "Let there be no more me but you shining through me," I became immune to all pain because I am no longer there but the Almighty above who is taking all the punishments.

The money my parents paid him for the car was not enough for a down payment for a new car and he needed five thousand pesos more. Despite his blatant discourse of how much more he cared for his fraternity brothers than my family and me, he shamelessly came to me once more for help. I was still hoping that kindness would bring Junn back to my children, that kindness would awaken him from his madness. I made a personal loan to help him again. Manang Fely, our Personnel Manager of the Real Estate Department at SSS was my guarantor for my loan. I never told anyone about this because I am sure anyone who would hear what I did would think I am the dumbest of all, but I did it because I was still hoping that kindness would bring Junn back to my children. I did it out of desperation for my children to have their father back. I was willing to buy him back if that was what it would take to make my family whole again for my children's sake.

Junn bought a brand-new car from the five thousand pesos which I borrowed to give him. It was a red Lancer. I bought golden sticky monograms and spelled my name and my three children's name on the glove compartment. I was legally the rightful owner of that car too even if Junn would pay me back my money which he never did. Yolanda had removed my name on the glove compartment, exactly as I expected. The car ended up for the exclusive use of Junn and Yolanda until the flame of their lust for each other was extinguished by another femme fatale, Vilma.

CHAPTER 7

More Trials in My Life

I continued to request for all the away assignments at work. Going to the different Islands in the Philippines was a good therapy that helped to ease the pain. These away inspections lasted only three days at most anyway. The first and the last days were traveling days, and the middle day was the inspection day. I saw my children in the morning before I left and, in the evening, when I came home so the away inspections did not really take me away from my children too long each time, just a little over a day. These away assignments were always conducted during working days when the children were in school, and I was always home to be with them during weekends. And it only happened at most, once a month. I had trusted maids and Mama and Apang were in close proximity that I did not worry about them when I was away. I sometimes wondered why the other Appraisers did not vie with me to get those away inspections. It was a very good way of seeing the rest of our country. Perhaps they had been with SSS to long that they already had done these away inspections before or is it because of other unsavory reason, I wonder.

Edna and I became very close friends. She was also separated from her husband. There were times when we went to the park together with our children. She also had three children. My children were two boys and a girl, hers were two girls and a boy so the six of them had a good time romping about at the park together. One-time Edna and I headed for home together after work. She invited me to have dinner with her. We did not plan it; the idea just came out of the blue so off we went to her apartment. We had a lengthy heart to heart talk. She asked me to stay overnight, and she gave me a very pretty delicate pink nightie to wear to sleep, which I have kept as a souvenir from Edna, and it is still in my sleepwear drawer until now. I trusted her enough to reveal to her my encounter with the manifestations of the evil force. I did not feel free to tell anyone about that dreadful ordeal, but Edna was an intellectual and I wanted to know how she would react and what she would think about my encounter. To my surprise, she told me she also had experienced something that cannot be explained by science. I was relieved and at the same time delighted to know that we both had paranormal encounters.

It was such a big relief that I was finally able to vent out to someone the whole ordeal, to someone with sympathetic ears who understood and who believed every word I said. It felt so good to have gotten it all out of my chest after I had bottled it up for three years. I told her how this demonic force took control of my own hands and how my own hands came up to my neck against my will to strangle myself when it failed to turn me into a murderer through its demonic urgings. I told her that I believed it was through divine intervention that I was saved from dying from my own hands, which would have been blamed on Junn who was sleeping next to me. I did not tell her about other visions that I saw, because at that time I still did not know what they meant but I was thinking about them. I kept thinking of one vision where I saw some kind of wave of energy emanating from each person on earth, which joined together as one. I could not make any sense of the vision. In fact, I could not make sense of all the visions I saw so I decided not to tell Edna about them at all. She believed my story about the manifestation of evil spirits on me because of her own unexplainable experience. She had an out of body experience, which she shared with me, and I believed every word she said. I guess only the people who had experienced a paranormal phenomenon are the people who can believe our stories. I understand fully because I could not believe these kinds of stories either until I had experienced it.

Edna said that every night before going to sleep she would go to her children's room to see if they all had fallen asleep. She lay down on her bed one night and when she got rested enough, she got up to check if her children were already sleeping. She wanted to turn off the electric fan because her room had cooled down enough but the fan would not go off. She started to think, "What is wrong with this fan? Is it broken?" She did not notice readily that her fingers were just going right through the fan switches without deactivating it. She gave up trying to turn the fan off and went towards her door and tried to open it to get to the next room. She could not turn the knob and when her hand slipped, her hand went through the door, and she realized that she could just actually go right through the solid closed door. She started to get alarmed when, at the corner of her eyes, she saw someone lying down on her bed. She looked and she saw that she was the one lying down on her bed; there were two of them in her room. She got very worried and started thinking, "Am I dead? Am I my soul and that is my physical body?" She said that she was tempted go through the closed door to check her children, but she said she could not accept to be dead, thinking, "Who would take care of my children?" She went back to where her physical body was lying and tried to reunite her two selves together. Her concern grew when she lifted one of her arms to see if she was one whole being again, with her physical body and soul together, but her physical arm did not move. She tried several times unsuccessfully when suddenly there was a sort of snap and boom; she was back as one entity again. She was so relieved that she was still physically alive for her children's sake.

Like me, she was also very relieved that she was able to get her story out of her chest. She could not tell it anyone. My brother, Nonoy had a similar experience when he was seventeen. He told me that it was always hard for him to get up in the morning when his body was still too sleepy, but the alarm clock was telling him it was time to get ready for school. So, one morning, he counted one, two, three and up, with full force he pulled himself up. Suddenly there were two of them; his conscious self was up but his physical body was still lying down asleep. He said he lifted his spirit feet and started to stroke his motionless physical feet. He got tempted to try to float around when he suddenly got pulled back to his physical body and that was the end of his out of body episode. When Nonoy told me about his experience, I had not experienced my ordeal with the spirits yet and I had wondered if he was just dreaming. I believe him now. Edna and Nonoy are two people I know personally who had experienced an out of body phenomenon.

Fe, the lady Appraiser who repeatedly told everybody that she was an unbending, strict and righteous Appraiser, had been flaunting precious jewelry that she had been buying. She asked me a favor. Since she was my trainer when I was a newcomer, I had always felt that I owed her something and I thought that it would be nice to be able to return the favor. She asked me to sign the report that she had written for her inspection of a house. She handed me the case folder and I saw that she was the Appraiser of the last two inspections of this same house. Inspecting a house two consecutive times was discouraged in our department. She told me that she had already gone to the site and everything was in order. She told me that the house was ninety five percent complete on her third inspection. She did all the necessary calculations for the third inspection, and she had written all the recommendations. All I had to do was to affix my signature in her hand-written report. Her previous report indicated that the house was ninety percent complete. I thought that it was safe enough to consent to her request, anyway five- percent discrepancy would be easy enough to rectify. I agreed to sign her third report that the house was ninety five percent complete, and I estimated that the money that would be released would only amount to about five thousand pesos.

It was my intention to verify the report the following day so that if anything was amiss, I would retrieve Fe's report, which I signed, and delete my signature from it before any more funds were released from the loan. Unfortunately, I came down with the flu the following day and I was too sick to finish all my inspection. I was in bed for three days. One Building Contractor who regularly follows up loan releases for his clients, heard that I was sick. He visited me at home to see how I was doing on the third day I was out from work. I was feeling better. We talked about things he was interested in. He told me about his on-going quest to find some treasures rumored to have been buried by General Yamashita in the Philippines during the Second World War. His eagerness for this treasure hunt was so apparent by the way he told me his story. He said that they had dug up some kind of a very thick concrete structure very deep below the ground which was very promising and that they were in the process of procuring all the necessary equipments to get through this concrete barrier. I never found out the result of his treasure hunting pursuit because to encourage friendship with these Building Contractors was inappropriate for a person in my position.

Our conversation started heading to another topic and then he started to warn me about the Building Contractor Fe had been hanging out with. They nicknamed this Contractor Bigote for his thick bushy mustache. He warned me that words were going around that Bigote had squandered the money released from the SSS housing loan and the house was abandoned. I suddenly thought of the report Fe had asked me to sign. I suddenly remembered that I failed to verify if the report I signed was accurate. A foreboding feeling crept inside me. I asked my visitor to please take me to the site of the house he was talking about. This kind friendly contractor agreed without any hesitation and while we were driving towards the site, I was praying so hard hoping that this abandoned construction site is not the same one of which progress report Fe had asked me to sign. He was so kind to give me a round-trip ride.

I was horrified when I saw the condition of the abandoned construction site. To my great dismay and horror, the general configuration of the house could very well be the one I signed for Fe, which she reported to be ninety percent complete on her second report, and which she told me was ninety five percent complete on her third inspection, but it did not have a roof nor a floor slab. All it had were block walls on footings, tie beams and roof rafters, nothing else. The soil where the slab would be poured was not even leveled yet and it was not at all ready for the concrete slab pouring. I tried to assure myself that it could not be the same house Fe got me involved with. Fe could never do anything so horrendous to me. But it was on the same Subdivision site, which made my apprehension to mount but I tried to hide it from the kind contractor who brought me to the site. I could not allow anybody to know that there was the possibility that I had committed such a stupid blunder. I took note what street the abandoned site was on and which particular lot it was.

As soon as I got to work the following morning I went to the Records Section and asked for that particular case folder. As soon as I saw the address of the case file, I knew I was in deep deep trouble. I hoped that I could still stop the loan money recommended from the report I signed from being released but I found out that it was too late. The loan amount recommended based on the report was already released. Fe must have pulled all the strings she could pull to have the money released within three days after I signed the report. How could Fe do such a horrible thing to me? Even her first report was not justified by the condition of the construction. She fooled me to sign for her that it was ninety five percent complete. A friend whom I trusted had betrayed me. She was aware of the problems I was going through in my life, and she deliberately implicated me in her crime. I could not believe that she could be so ruthless. What did I do to her to deserve such cruelty; I was trying to rationalize her motivation for doing such a heinous deed, but I could not come up with any valid rationalization.

I could not tell Edna how stupid I was to allow Fe to implicate me with her crime. I could not even confront Fe about the horrendous catastrophe she got me into. I could not blame anyone but myself. I was lost; I did not know what to do. The consequence of the crime was unbearable to think of. Aside from getting dismissed dishonorably from my job, all my college work would be for nothing if I lost my license as an

Architect. I should not let this worry me, remember, there is no more self to be hurt, I reminded myself, but it was easier said than done because this time it was more than my ego that was hurt.

My inspection assignment for that day was with Rene, a trusted friend from the Credit Division who was like a brother to everyone. Before we left the SSS building for our field inspection, I told Rene that I had a humongous problema. I am sure that he could tell by my demeanor that I was in real trouble. There was an open landscaped courtyard in the middle of the SSS building complex with a nice bench where Rene invited me to sit down with him. In a warm brotherly tone he told me, "Come, let us sit down and tell me what your problema is". I confided to him my predicament. Rene listened patiently and, in the end, I said, "Oh Rene, what shall I do?" I was so distraught. Rene advised me that the only recourse was to tell Atty. Baybay the truth.

Atty. Baybay, my very kind and compassionate Division Chief, who in the past had always shown concern for my well-being, was very understanding. He understood my predicament and he was furious with Fe. There was no question about my allegation because all the three reports obviously were Fe's handwriting except that my signature was affixed on the last report. He called Fe and Bigote for an emergency meeting. Atty. Baybay came up with a solution to save me from dishonor, but I had to pay a high price for my misdemeanor. I never found out what Fe and Bigote contributed to this solution. All I was told was that I had to put in sixteen thousand pesos, more than three times the amount released from Fe's report, which I signed, to get the house constructed according to the report that I signed. It was my punishment for trusting someone I thought was my friend. Sixteen thousand pesos was the equivalent of eight months' work. It was the duty of Atty. Baybay as division chief to make the necessary disciplinary steps against Fe and myself as soon as the case was laid on his desk but his compassion for me prevailed. He risked his own position when he gave us this alternative solution that would save us from dishonor. So, he demanded that the process to correct the anomaly be done immediately. There was no time to wait for Bigote to come up with the full amount needed. I had to put in the needed balance to finish the task within the allotted time. Atty. Baybay himself took the necessary measures to make sure the construction was done.

I was a blessing in disguise to the homeowner, whoever he was. Had I not gotten involved in this case, the owner would have gotten in a swindling lawsuit against Bigote. Fe would have been dismissed dishonorably and she would have lost her Architect's license. Atty. Baybay demanded that Fe hand in her resignation immediately. He could not file a case against Fe for corruption without getting me involved because I was the last to sign the report and by doing so, I corroborated all of Fe's previous reports. I wondered if Fe deliberately got me involved as a way of saving her Architect's license.

The house was constructed to uphold my report and Atty. Baybay let my misdemeanor go unreported. My record remained untainted. Fe was forced to resign from her post. Her crime was wiped away when the house was brought up to the status of the report. All I lost was money, sixteen thousand hard earned pesos. I was so thankful for having such a compassionate Division Chief, Atty. Baybay, I did not know how to thank him enough. He saved me my hard-earned Architect's license, which is priceless.

After a few months, a Davao assignment came up. As usual I volunteered. Davao like Cotabato was also in the island of Mindanao, the second biggest island of the Philippines in the south where people are predominantly Moslem. I knew Fe was from Davao. I took her address from our records before I took my trip. At Davao, when my task was done, I searched for Fe and I found her. I wanted to see her because I could not stop feeling sorry for her for what happened. I wanted to know how she was doing. She had lost a front tooth. I wondered if she was hurting for money that she could not have the tooth replaced, but of course I would not ask. The fact that I found her at home during working hours was not a good indication either. Her manner was aloof, but I could read the unspoken apology on her face, she could not look at me in the eye. She probably thought that I came to ask her to pay me back the money I lost.

I never really confronted Fe about the whole fiasco that got us both in big trouble and made her lose her appraiser job. Down deep in my heart the real reason why I searched for her was my unexplainable compassion for someone who had fallen. I wanted to see her get up again. I wanted her to know that I was still her friend despite what happened, and that everything was forgiven. I never let loss of material things bother me, that is why I have no need for jewelry because I don't like to worry about loosing them. I lost money many times, but it is just money, which I can make again. Feeling bad about losing money would only aggravate my emotional turmoil and I don't allow that to bother me. I am sure that this is what Jesus meant when he said leave all your material possessions, come and follow me. He did not mean turn yourself into paupery and be a burden to others, he meant don't allow material possessions to weigh you down with miserable tormenting worries, which only keep you from finding inner peace. That is the most valuable treasure that I have, inner peace. In spite of all the adversities that have come my way, deep within me, I have peace and I am really happy within, enjoying the rewards of a clear conscience, knowing I have not done anything wrong to anyone whether in thoughts or in action.

When I got back to the main office, I told everyone I saw Fe. They all asked me if she had given me her jewelry that she used to flaunt around to make up for what she did to me. I smiled at them in response. How could I make them understand that my visit to Fe was not intended to be a confrontational one? In retrospect I began to remember that she was not wearing any jewelry at all when I saw her. Was she really financially hurting that she had sold all of her jewelry that she was so proud of? Casting my burden to a higher up really works. Whatever Fe did to me did not really hurt me at all. All I could feel was compassion for her.

One afternoon, I went back to the office after my inspections to write all my reports so that the following day I could go straight to my site inspection duties first hour in the morning. After I finished my reports, I noticed that everyone had left the office for the day except Filo. He offered to give me a ride home. I happily accepted his offer; I would save on a taxi fare. He was a very charming fellow, and I was really very fond of him in a friendly way. We were both members of the SSS choir and we had sung many duets before. We got into his car, and I buckled myself up on the passenger seat but when I turned to look at him, he put his arm around my neck, and he pulled me close to him and passionately kissed me. He caught me completely off-guard. I found his other hand while he was kissing me and held onto it tightly with both my hands before he could start groping me. He told me, "I will not take you home yet. I'm taking you to a motel."

"You're not going to rape me, are you?" I wearily asked.

"Don't you need it?" He asked me with a puzzled look in his face surprised that his charm did not disarm me. He released me from his hold and placed both his hands back on the car steering wheel.

"Look Filo, we're both married. Right now, I go to bed in peace knowing that I have not broken any law. If I break the law, I will lose my inner peace as well. That's when I would really be lost. I can't afford to lose my inner peace because it is the only thing I have." I know that Junn had freed me from our marital vows, but I made a vow to God never to cause another wife the pain that my adulterous husband and his paramour had inflicted to me.

"What do you do at night, hug a pillow? Is that enough for you?" It sounded so funny the way he said it with a comical face. Filo had become such a dear friend to me I could never get angry with him.

How can I explain that I didn't really feel alone at night? How can I explain that ever since I got my little book, The Imitation of Christ, I have gradually developed a connection with a sort of an energy giving force, which presence became so real, a real warm comforting energy that envelopes me in my solitude filling my heart with joy and I really never felt alone in my bed at night or anywhere I go. The truth was that I felt this comforting presence every time I direct my thoughts towards Jesus, the true source of my strength. I only had to think that if Jesus carried his cross, who am I not to carry mine. This comforting presence puts me to sleep in a silent sweet lullaby every night and I never felt lacking. Of course, I could not tell Filo what was going on in my mind. I did not want him to think that I was being melodramatic so I just said, "What else can I do, that's how my life is."

There was silence. Then he said, "Alright, I'll take you home," His concern sounded sincere.

I thought he was cute to be concerned. His attempt to give me some comfort, in the manner he knew how to give comfort, did not make me feel like I was violated but instead I took it more as a compliment, a sort of an assurance that I was still desirable which was sort of an ego booster for me, a reminder that I was just a mere human.

The following morning Filo could not look at me, in fact he was avoiding me. I knew he was embarrassed by what he did the previous night. I quietly walked to his desk when he wasn't looking and touched him gently on his head, "How is my friend today?" I tried to convey to him with the tone of my voice that I did not mind what he did. I knew he was trying to do me a favor. I did not tell a soul about this incident until now that I am writing about it. Filo did not need to worry about me. Every night I slept peacefully because of that comforting presence that comes to me when I am alone but there was still a wound in my heart that needed to heal. I couldn't tell if the pain in my heart was really the fear of what my broken marriage would do to the development of my three little children whom I love so dearly but I knew time heals all wounds. I knew that in time the pain in my heart would fade away, the only question was when. It is really hard to explain why I did not feel truly alone. I somehow had broken through a barrier of some sort and established a connection with something great and wonderful that I could not explain, and it gave me tranquility.

A childhood friend surprised me with a telephone call one day. It was Ato, my dear friend from my youth. He brought back to my mind all my memories of my visits to Iriga, the Burabod, a pristine pond that was so enchantingly beautiful at the foot of Iriga Mountain, with its cool fresh water naturally fed by a natural spring coming out between huge boulders. Lush ferns and wild plants with beautiful flowers naturally grew on the surroundings adding a magical touch to the scenery that looked like the dwelling place of fairies. This beautiful pond had boulders strewn everywhere where we could climb and jump into the clean, fresh clear water, you could see the bottom. A huge acacia tree with its canopy of stretched out branches filled with thick foliage kept the pond shaded. Some boys climbed up the Acacia branches and jumped down to the water making a huge splash. It was there where I first learned to swim when I was seven. I always felt I was in an enchanted garden every time I was at Burabod and as a child, I daydreamed of being at Burabod many a times because the thought of being in such a beautiful place, one of Mother Nature's masterpieces, made me feel that I was in paradise.

Ato also made me remember the exciting trek to Mt. Iriga, and the bowling games at the Alatco Playhouse with our other teenage friends. Being remembered by an old friend from my childhood whom I have not seen for several years was such a pleasant surprise. I invited him to come and see me. I had not seen him for so long. He was the young sixteen-year-old lad who told me he loved me the last time we met at Iriga and he said he would wait for me. I was so mean to him. I flatly told him that he was waiting for nothing, unmindful of his feelings. I thought it would be nice to renew our friendship. My cousin who still lives in Iriga must have given him my telephone number.

I went out to dinner with him. We had a long talk reminiscing about all the fun things we did when we were teenagers in Iriga. I did not feel obligated to hide from him the tragic end of my marriage. He in turn told me about some business endeavor he was engaged in but his finances did not meet what was needed and that he must come up with a couple more thousand pesos to close the deal otherwise he would lose all the initial money he had already invested in the transaction. It was close to Christmas again. I got my bonus from SSS. I lent him my whole bonus of two thousand pesos to help him get out of his predicament. I trusted that he would return the money to me when his business transaction went through. I had all the Christmas presents for my children; I thought I could spare that money to help an old friend and also to make up for treating him so unkindly that last time we saw each other two decades ago.

A few months later he came back. He needed more money. When I told him that I did not have any more money to give, his tone of voice changed, and he forcefully continued to demand that I give him more money. What happened to him, his abrupt change was a big surprise for me. Of course, I would not give him any more money. I lent him my money because I wanted to help him. I was expecting him to pay me back when his business transaction went through. I was so naïve; I fell for his trickery. My trusting nature made me gullible once again to a con artist. I could not believe Ato had become a con artist. He threatened to make a story to Junn if I did not give him more money. He turned into an extortionist. Why should I care what story he told Junn. If he thought, he could blackmail me he was awfully mistaken. He roughly held my chin in his one hand while his other big heavy hand tapped on my cheek, acting like a real gangster from the movies. He was hurting me. He then held my hand and took my college ring from my finger. Ato was a very strong muscular man I knew it was futile to wrestle with him to get my ring back. I asked him to leave but he did not heed my words. I knew he would not leave so I left, and I started walking towards my parents' home on the other side of the block. He followed me but as soon as I got inside my parents' home, I locked the door. Ato could not dare carry on with his gangster-like demeanor at my parent's home. He tried to make my young brother Oyet open the door with a friendly bidding through the window. I was glad my young brother was sensible enough not to let him in. I did not go home until he had gone. I never saw Ato again after that.

Ato was another big disappointment for me. An old friend whom I trusted to be honorable turned out to be an evil extortionist. Was that his revenge because I rejected him when we were young? He had taken my college ring. It has my name in it. I suddenly remembered that at the time I was having those mysterious ordeals, I heard a voice who asked me that if I can take a physical object to the hereafter, which would I take and I said my college ring because at that time it was the most valuable possession I had because the ring was the symbol of all my efforts to become an Architect. So, it happened that the only material thing that I valued was lost. These people who seem to have ganged up on me to break my spirit made me think of the story of Job, but nothing could break me now after I have overcome the most horrendous ordeal that could possibly confront any human. I got used to being a spectator of how people do their follies. The purpose of life is to be happy. What does anyone gain from deceit? Is it to bring them happiness? Without a clear conscience how can anyone be happy? Don't they know that inner peace is the main ingredient to attain happiness and inner peace will never be attained with guilt? I lost money again. I reminded myself once again of the lesson of Jesus about material possessions. It is sad that both Fe's and Ato's dignity has a price. When someone has a price for his or her dignity, he or she is a pathetic being who is still very low in the evolution progress. All I could feel for them is pity. I forgave all of them for what they did to me because if I did not forgive them, the resulting emotion would be vengeance which would only take away my inner peace and no one can rob me of my inner peace for as long as I walk on the path that Jesus laid for me to follow. For as long as my children and I are not deprived of whatever we need, losing the money did not matter to me. Money is just a means to an end. I can always make the money I lost. I must admit it is sad that I once again witnessed someone's downfall. A few years later, I heard Ato was dead. I didn't bother to ask how he met his demise.

I really believed Vilma's sincerity. The construction of the house that was built for my family financed by our SSS loan had long been finished and unoccupied for a year or so because I did not want to move into it. Junn had decided to live with Yolanda and not with us, why would I move to that house and be far away from my parents? Junn must have told Vilma about this house because she persuaded me to move into it with the promise that if I did, Junn would start coming home to me and my children and my family would be whole again. She said our apartment was right next to where my parents and relatives were and Junn was not comfortable being near them. Of course, he would not be comfortable to be near where with my loved ones were, the way he was behaving. Nara and Marilyn did not move with us, but Nita took their place. Virgie learned to sew from the sewing lessons I gave her, and I was happy to see her become a seamstress. I regret making the move because Junn did not keep his promise and because in this new location, Junn was uninhibited to conduct whatever illicit activity he wanted to do when I was not home.

Back at work, I got another surprise call again. It was Yolanda, I did not expect that she would ever call me again after Junn told me in front of her that he was moving out of our home to be with her. She wanted me to meet her again at the restaurant where we had met before. I was curious what she had to say, and I am really a person who finds it so hard to say no to anyone, so I agreed to see her. She was wearing black. She was in mourning. She told me that misfortune had struck her family. Her father had fallen from a tree and died, and her younger sister was fatally run over by a car. Two deaths had come to her. I wondered why she was telling me about her tragedies. Did she want my sympathy, or did her guilt drive her to let me know that she had been punished? Was I supposed to take this gesture as an unspoken apology? She said that Vilma had come between her and Junn. I told her. "I warned you that Junn is fickle. Did you think that you could change him?" I felt sorry for her, but I couldn't believe what she said that Vilma had come between her and Junn, how could that be? Vilma was doing everything to help my family be whole again. Should I tell Yolanda that she was mistaken? Would I be telling a lie if I told her that Junn was back with his legal family?

Yolanda's baby boy meant responsibility crept into Junn's life again, which, in my observation, was not welcome in his life and it extinguished his lust for Yolanda so he had to look for another woman who would make him feel that burning passionate lust once again. This time, could it really be Vilma who was conveniently there, a married woman? Could she possibly reciprocate Junn's lust for a new bed partner? People working with Junn and Vilma in the Oil distributing Company were starting to notice something going on between them and they were getting annoyed. Because of Vilma's insistence, Junn had taken me to his company's social functions, so I had met all the people he worked with. One lady in their firm called me and asked me to come to their office for a meeting to discuss something very important. They wanted me to stop whatever was going on between Vilma and Junn. I trusted that Vilma was sincerely honest to me, and I thought that these people they worked with in their office were misinformed. I thought that Vilma was truly trying to mend my broken marriage. The lady who invited me to the meeting, I can't remember her name anymore, turned against me because I would not cooperate with her and because I was in fact defending Vilma. This lady was so annoyed that she started berating me.

A few days later, Nita told me that Junn had brought Vilma to our new home and she told me that they acted like lovers when they thought she was not looking. It was another disappointment. Did Vilma sincerely try to put back together my broken marriage or was she merely using me to take Junn away from Yolanda so that she could possess Junn for herself? She knew I was not her competition; she knew it was Yolanda. But she was a married woman and a mother of a little boy. How could she jeopardize her own marriage? I confronted Junn about this for Vilma's sake, I did not want to see another marriage broken, especially where the life of another baby boy was going to be adversely affected. When I asked, "Does her husband know about this?" His response was, "He loves her too much." Did he mean that Vilma's husband was willing to watch her wife do her fling until their burning lust was over? He must truly love her.

One day, Yolanda saw Junn's red car parked outside a restaurant. She went inside the restaurant, and she found Junn with Vilma. Enraged with jealousy, she took the glass of soda on the table and poured it on Vilma's head. Vilma on the other hand grabbed Yolanda's little finger and bit it as hard as she could it almost got decapitated. The two women got into an embarrassing brawl in the restaurant. A policeman came to stop their fight. Junn brought the two women to our new home, which was the closest place they could conveniently take refuge to settle their volatile dispute so that they would come to a peaceful truce. Raqui and Tentong were at home at that time, but they were too young to understand what was going on.

I heard the story from Nita as soon as I got home from work. I got furious. The nerve of these immoral beings conducting their illicit hanky punky business in my home was infuriating and to carry on in front of my daughter and son was so disgusting I was boiling mad with anger. But anger is a negative emotion that would only make my body produce free radicals and if I allow that to happen, then I would be the loser and with this thought I calmed myself down. I started to imagine the circus of comedy of two women in a brawl over my husband in a public place with a policeman pulling them apart and I found myself laughing at what must have been a very hilarious scenario. The two women fought against each other over my husband. Why didn't they attack Junn who was the one victimizing them? These were the kind of women that boosted Junn's ego, women who were tigers. I saw that his arm looked like he was scratched by a tiger. He had deep parallel wounds on his arm when he visited the children one time. I bet they were caused by Yolanda's fingernails since she was the woman scorned this time. These women seem to be trying to out do each other on who can get to the lowest level of immorality. I do not really believe that love was the motivator for these unending love triangles in Junn's life. Many call it love, I call it lust. Love is a deeper sublime feeling, which is unselfish, and which has the willingness to sacrifice. Love is giving, caring, uncompromising and never taking. The two women got into a brawl because they wanted to possess Junn. It was a selfish motive that made them forget about maintaining a civilized decorum. It was their lust for Junn that got them into a brawl, what a shame and how lowly they had become, how disgraceful. If they love Junn they should have conceded that Junn should be home with his true family, with his children because that is the only way Junn would attain his inner peace and theirs too. Unfortunately, their moral weakness clouded their reasoning, and their lust dictated their actions, a typical trait of an animal. In the end, both Junn and Vilma were terminated from the Oil Distributing Company for adultery. Once again Junn found another woman to replace both Vilma and Yoly. After Junn's successful lung surgery, he gained weight, and I must admit he became good looking that these lustful women of low morality were easy prey.

CHAPTER 8

Goodbye Beloved Land of My Birth

My sister Anita, who is six years younger than me, after being a nurse for five years in America, came for a visit. It was a very happy occassion for all of us. She got married to a Chilean named Paul, who migrated to the US. He is a handsome tall blue-eyed redhead fellow. Anita showed everyone his photograph, which she carried in her wallet. We were all very happy for her. She was doing very well in America.

Mama and Apang followed Anita to America a month after she left. They spent Christmas with her. My children and I stayed at their home while they were gone because I still had three teenage brothers that I had to look after. They came home from America with the news that Anita was pregnant. Mama was very worried that Anita would have her baby with no one to help her. She did not have any relatives in America. Mama started persuading me to go to America to be with my sister when she had her baby. I suspected another reason why she was pushing me to go to America, she was probably trying to give me a chance for a different life in a country where there is divorce.

I decided that if I was going to leave my children with my parents while I was away, we might as well continue living with them until I leave so that by that time, the children would be used to living at my Mama and Apang's household. They were used to my parent's home already but just for visits and not as residents. It was a very good excuse to stay away from Junn. I gave up trying to mend our rift. I left all the material possessions that I have acquired over the years to Junn, all furniture, appliances, home decors, china wares, glass wares, everything except the children's and my clothing. The piano was the only heavy item plus the set of encyclopedia books and my original Bible that I moved to my parent's home for the children.

I needed our income tax return to show the American Consulate that I could afford to be a tourist. I asked Junn for the papers. Every time he came to see the children, he would say he forgot to bring them. I went to his office and asked for the papers. I told him, "I'm not leaving without the papers." The documents were on his attaché case all along, which he carried with him anywhere he went. He finally handed them to me. I found out the real reason why he could not give me our tax papers. He had declared his son with Yolanda in our tax returns. That was how I came to know that their baby was named Vladimir, and he was born on the same day as my youngest son, Tentong's birthday. I could not declare that I have four children, so I had the papers redone without the fourth child in it through an SSS friend that has a tie with the Bureau of Internal Revenues, BIR.

When I arrived at the U.S. Embassy in Manila, I was greeted by the sight of a very long line of people queuing to get inside the building. It was my very first attempt to get a visa. I did not expect that it would be such a hassle. The line looked like a mile long to me; I almost backed out, "How on earth can all these people get inside the building before sundown?" I thought. Before I could turn around to leave, a little girl approached me. She spoke so softly, she said, "My mother is on the line," she pointed to her mother who waved at us. I saw that she was very close to the entrance of the building. "She will give you her spot for fifty pesos," the little girl said to me. I felt so sorry for the little girl. Her mother must have been standing on that line since dawn. These poor people would do anything to make a living. I gave the little girl fifty pesos and she led me to her mother who gave me her place on the queue. I heard all sorts of begrudged comments, which I decided to ignore. I was thinking that I would never do this again anyway.

Inside the Embassy building, I took a seat on the waiting room. There were a lot of other people ahead of me. It would be a long wait. I started thinking of all other people who had left the Philippines to find a greener pasture abroad. I never really had any intention of leaving my country. I had thought that one of the problems of my country was that it was getting brain drained. Almost everyone who got educated and who finished college applied for immigration to the U.S. In fact, the choice of the field of educational pursuit of almost every high school graduate was dictated by whatever profession was in demand in the U.S. Why do we have to leave, I thought, why can't we make our country better instead?

I started thinking of all the corruption I had personally witnessed and heard of in my country. I know corruption happens not only in the government but even within private sectors as well. My mind started to wander back to a big disappointment I had encountered at work more than a decade ago, during the late sixties, the big Architectural competition for the design of a complex that would house the Asian Development Bank and the United Nations Headquarters in Manila. All leading Architects in the Philippines participated in the competition. I was working at the office of Architect Eseng, one of the competitors. I started working in this company while I was still an Architectural student at M.I.T. I was among a team of other young Architects to do all the presentation drawings of the design. Nani was our job captain. Our team had to move to another secret site so that we could concentrate on the challenging task of putting together our design package. This set up also allowed the regular functions and activities of the main office to continue unhindered by the competition preparation activities.

We all worked so diligently with full dedication. The spirit of competition brought out the best in all of us. We even competed against each other, trying to out do one another in producing perfect presentation drawings without any blemishes or errors. Those were the days when computer aided drafting was still unheard of in the Philippines. All Floor Plans, Elevations and Sections had to be manually drawn by pen and ink on illustration boards. All of us meticulously drew all the necessary pen and ink drawings as skillfully as we could. When the two-dimensional drawings were substantially completed, a crew of scaled model makers came to join us. We wanted to win, the thrill of competition was so exciting, and the pitch of our anxiety grew feverish as the deadline for submission of our entry drew closer. We knew we had to finish our work in time at all cost and we were all willing to work overnight if it was necessary.

The presentation was done all in black and white. Even the scaled model of the complex was all in white with a touch of different gradations pf greens for the landscape. All entries to the competition were supposed to be incognito. There should be no identifying mark whatsoever that would give any clue as to the identity of the designing Architectural firm. It was a measure that was taken to insure fairness in judging. A board of judges was formed composed of "reputable" high-ranking personalities in the Philippines and the Chairman of the Board was the Dean of the college of Architecture of the University of the Philippines.

Finally, our design package was completed a week before the deadline of submission. We were all very happy with the outcome of our combined dedicated efforts. We knew we had a big chance to win, and our anxiety grew each day as we continued to work diligently until the project was completed and ready for submission to the competition. On the day before our entry was delivered to the designated site of competition, Herrmencita Unso, our office secretary whom we called Baby Unso came to our drafting room and announced, "Guys, guess who is in our conference room right at this very moment? The Dean of

Architecture of the University of the Philippines, the Chairman of the Board of Judges for the competition."

No way, it could not be, we all poured out our energy with all our hearts and worked so hard for this competition. We were all so confident that the design we produced would win and we all thought that rigging the competition was unnecessary. I wanted to see it for myself. I could not believe Baby Unso. I dashed towards the conference room where the complete design with the scaled model of our entry was displayed, and I was dismayed to see the man who was not supposed to be there seated on a chair at the end of the long conference table. No! No! No! I was so appalled. It was a tremendous heart-breaking disappointment.

Our Architectural firm won the competition, which was rigged for the glory of Architect Eseng. The commission of designing the Asian Bank and the United Nations Headquarter Complex was awarded to our office. There were champagne bottles popping up to celebrate the occasion but there was no jubilation among us who produced the presentation drawings. That night, the whole staff involved in the preparation of the presentation package for the competition decided to gather at Baby Unso's home to comfort one another. None of us were in the mood to talk, we were all so quiet. It was a very somber gathering more fitted for a funeral, devoid of any feeling of euphoria for winning a competition. We were robbed of our dignity, and we were all mourning our loss. I lost my enthusiasm for my work, but I could not resign. Junn needed medical attention. I needed my job, but I knew I could not stay on my job much longer. Leaving my profession to stay home and be a mother while sewing clothes for a living became an easy decision to make after that.

I felt so guilty for being such a coward. Could I have made a difference if I had come forward to thwart the rigged judging? Rumors had it that all the judges were in cahoots. Architect Eseng did not care for the award money, so the award money was distributed among the judges. What Architect Eseng wanted was the honor and prestige. He would not be doing all the construction documents for free; it was a huge undertaking and the compensation for the designer was a fortune. It would have been my word, a mere nobody, against all those big named judges. Nestor, Eseng's brother was married to the daughter of Senator Laurel, was the Senator involved in this hideous corruption? I hope not. I would surely have landed in jail for slander if I revealed what I knew to a news reporter. I am no hero but a mere shameful coward who watched the corruption happen without doing anything to prevent it.

My mind continued to wander to another rumor I heard when I attended an annual gathering of Pilipino Architects. I heard that the Architect of a big Project in Manila had a nervous breakdown; he could not take the aftermath of a big catastrophe. Scaffolding had collapsed and had buried numerous laborers alive. The First Lady did not allow rescue operation because there was no time. A big World event, the Miss Universe Pageant was being hosted in Manila. She would be facing a big embarrassment internationally if the venue would not be ready for the big event. But what about the poor workers who had been buried under the debris, they could still be alive! The big decision was made that no rescue operations will be done! There was no time for it! Fill everything with concrete and be done with it, the First Lady ordered. Why did I hear rumors like that? Why was there no media cover of the event on television or in the newspaper? The NPA alleged that there was no freedom of the press. The President dictated what can be printed on the newspapers or broadcasted on radios and televisions. There was another fascist Filipino President who executed people without due process of law. The home of a medical doctor was forcefully broken in at three o'clock in the morning while everyone on that home were asleep and everybody were massacred, shot dead in their sleep because there was a suspected NPA who was a guest in that home. The President judged them all guilty without bothering to present evidence of their guilt. I don't see any redeeming quality on this fascist President, and I see him on his way to being cast to the lake of fire.

Then one of the strange visions that I saw while I was fighting against evil satanic forces, my sign of Jonah ordeal, before the year 1975 ended came back to my mind. I was floating close to the ceiling of the filing room of the Professional Board Examination Office, did I have an out of body experience? I saw a man in search of important documents, going over the Architectural Board examination papers, big sheets of tracing papers, where architectural plans were drawn by board examinees during the board examination. The man finally found what he was looking for and I instantly recognized that my board examination drawings were the object of his search. It was the design of a supermarket complex on a kilometer long lot, and it was so strange that I saw the man who seemed to be a clerk, changing the identification number of my examination papers. All board exam papers were supposed to be incognito just like the design competition for the ADB-UN complex. All examinees were not allowed to write their names on the examination papers and the examiners assigned identification numbers on our exam papers purportedly so that the board of examiners should judge the designs according to merit and not be influenced by the identity of the examinee. What was the vision telling me? I heard the voices of my college Instructors; I recognized their voices as they were deliberating over my exam papers. How I wish they would give light to the meaning of these visions; why was I given a glimpse of what goes on in the board examination filing room? Why was the identification number of my exam documents changed? Being the board exam topnotcher would give one a boost in his or her Architectural practice. A well-to-do schoolmate was declared the topnotcher of the board exam I took. I could not tell anyone about the vision that I saw because they would only say I have lost my mind. This Architectural exam topnotcher really didn't gain much from topping the board exam because he died before his Architectural career flourished. This reminded me of Ato who also died young after doing something wrong to me.

There were other visions about religious beliefs, which at that time I could not determine whether it was telling me the truth or if they were deceiving me because they were contrary to my religious indoctrination. Why were those visions given to me? Rumors had it that examinees with money bribe the Board of Examiners to assure them the honor of topping the Board examination as a career booster. Was it a higher entity who was communicating to me at that time, was it God? Did God give me those visions to confirm to me that the rumors were true? Was God telling me that none of these corruptions are hidden from Him? Woe to all of you corrupt people because all of you are guilty of stealing. You are taking dirty money and God knows about it.

Is there hope for my country? All poor nations have the same problems of corruptions, and this is true to all previous Spanish colonies. When Spain was a world power, the governors that were sent to the Spanish Colonies were the corrupt officials in the mainland who were being punished for their corruption and this to me, is one big reason why corruption is deeply rooted in all countries that were previous Spanish colonies and many, who never developed the patriotic love for the land of their birth, aspire to migrate to USA, illegally in most cases in South America. It is unfortunate that any politician who gets elected President in any poor nation has his priority set on enriching his pocket by corruption and by looting the government rather than sincerely serving the nation for the betterment of its people. I read a book about the negative effects of the World Bank and IMF do to third worlds. Is it really the World Bank and the IMF that are preventing the third world from accumulating capitals or is it because of the corrupt government officials who are pocketing kurakot money from the government that is causing the problem? Filipinos are educated people but why are they so dumb to keep on choosing movie or TV personalities to be the leaders of the nation? What do movie or TV personalities know about governing? The Bakya crowd does not care as long as they see their idols in the highest seat of the government. Elections in the Philippines are actually popularity contests, and the most popular idol gets elected regardless of whether he is competent enough to be the leader of the nation. They elect leaders for selfish reasons, for reasons that would give them personal benefits and they do not take into consideration the pertinent matters that would truly benefit the whole nation. Every election, tribalism always prevails. The island group that the Spaniards colonized into what is now the Philippines was never united but warring tribes that never got together peacefully.

I know of people who are true heroes. I know of people who -selflessly dedicated their lives to serve the poor but Filipino voters do not care to know about them because they are not interested in hard work that do not make them rich fast, so they do not have any admiration for these unknown true humanitarian people who truly cares about the welfare of the Filipinos. Filipinos are dreamers who would rather see their fantasies fulfilled by putting their movie idols in the highest political positions in the government and they pretend that they do not know that the only thing their idols are capable of doing is to rob the government.

There is my sister Elizabeth who became a doctor in the seventies but instead of building a lucrative career for herself in the city as what her peers did, she was up in the mountains giving medical care to the poor who had no means of paying her. I am very proud of her because she is one exceptional human being who is truly selfless. Other doctors did not waste any time migrating to the US for a better-quality life, but that idea was unthinkable for her. She devoted her time to the poor while she was young. She grew up in Manila, but she was willing to live in a place with no electricity, no telephone, no plumbing and no roads. From the bus depot, she had to hike at least seven kilometers on dangerous narrow trails up on the mountainsides that with one wrong step could send her to death plummeting down deep ravines. She learned to bathe on icy cold rivers and lived with the natives in the most primitive way and she did not mind because she loved the poor. She loved what she was doing, giving medical care to the poor. She truly loves the nation of her birth and migrating to another nation for her personal benefit never crossed her mind. She is a genuine follower of Jesus, and she does not even know it. She got married to another humanitarian doctor who, like her, was also serving the poor up in the mountains. Their humanitarian efforts caught the attention of some journalists and the story of their selfless dedication to their cause got published in some magazines, but Filipinos do not care about these kinds of stories. Filipinos think they are stupid to waste their time on the poor instead of making money with their professions because Filipinos have misguided values. If you are a native of the nation called Philippines and you believe you do not belong to my characterization of a Filipino then you are not a Filipino, you are perhaps a Pinoy whom I would hope would be one who truly loves his nation or perhaps you are one who does not know your identity. Anyway, the first Filipinos were Spaniards born in the Philippines, the indigenous natives were known as Indios.

People like my sister Elizabeth and her husband Ramon would be the perfect leader for this poor country because they would surely serve the people with full sincerity and dedication, and they would put all their energies towards the betterment of the nation with the assurance that they will not allow any corruption. But Filipinos would never idolize sincere people like Elizabeth and Ramon because they do not have any sense of sincerity in themselves and would never identify themselves with the likes of Elizabeth and Ramon. Filipinos would rather see an incompetent leader who is an entertainment celebrity. I know that Filipinos even defended a President from impeachment in spite of her apparent cheating, rigging the election to ensure her reelection because all Filipinos know that if they were in her shoes, they would do the same thing. That President was not a movie star, but she was just as popular as a movie star because she is the daughter of a past President and she was just pretty as any movie star and those are the qualities Filipino voters go for.

Waiting for my turn to be interviewed by the American Consul at the American Embassy really took a long time. My mind wandered back to my question of why Filipinos look for greener pastures abroad. Do they leave because they cannot fight the system, so they just leave or maybe because they have no love for their country at all? The only thing that motivates them is personal interest, selfish motives, anything that would give them material gains. Why do natives of the Philippines have this mentality? Is it because of the way they got educated? Is this the legacy of Western colonialism?

The Philippines is an agricultural nation, but farmers do not get the respect that they deserve, and they are exploited instead. There must be something wrong with the orientation of Philippine educational system, which is failing in inculcating into the minds of the people love for their nation. The root of the current Philippine educational system was planted by Americans, and it is lacking in instilling appreciation for what is native so that anyone who gets educated desires to leave the country and only a few intellectuals who furthers their education outside of the country's educational system becomes aware of who they really are. Elizabeth and Ramon are good examples of these few true lovers of their native land. Others who cannot tolerate the direction the country is going become militants and join the NPA.

While I was waiting to be interviewed at the US Embassy to acquire a visa, I asked myself, "Where do I fit in? I am here at the US Embassy seeking a visa. Am I leaving because I do not love my country? No, no, no, I am just going to visit my sister. I am coming back." My number was called. It was my turn to be interviewed by the American Consul. I got a visa allowing me to enter the United States. The next step was to resign from my work. Working for four years as an Appraiser at the Real Estate Department of the Philippine Social Security System was a very memorable one with all its ups and the downs. I was very sad to leave my friends at SSS. They gave me a going away luncheon party at a nearby restaurant. They had all been very kind to me. Whatever Fe did to me was all forgiven and I knew it was time to move on. I did not have intentions of making a career out of being an Appraiser. After working in a company for four years, you cannot avoid hearing some disappointing gossip about corruptions and what Fe did to me confirmed without any more doubts that it was indeed happening. Gossips about wives of overseas workers giving sexual favors to RED employees to expedite their loans did not bypass my ears either, which added to my disappointments. It is disheartening to admit that our generation has indeed become evil and adulterous.

The Visa I got was good for a year. I did not know how long I was going to stay in America. I know that to some people, looking for a job is a problem, but that was never my problem. I can always go back to sewing clothes if I needed to, but I would like to pursue a career in Construction when I come home. While I was an Appraiser, I had a chance to construct a few homes on the side and I enjoyed it. That was what I thought I would do when I came back. My children had always been very close to my parents and my brothers. I did not have to worry about them, but my problem was how long can I stay away from them. Just to think of leaving them even for just a month was breaking my heart. I have never been away from them for more than three days. But the call of adventure to America was irresistible and I had a mission to help my sister Anita have her baby.

Before I left for America, my good sister Mila, who is a certified public accountant took me out shopping for clothes and lingerie. Everything was on her. I remembered that during one of those days when Junn physically abused me, (he beat me up three times), Mila came to see me. She was feeling so sorry for me. She said, "I know you don't deserve this kind of life that you are having. Since we were little, I have not seen you do anything wrong. In fact, I would say you are a saint. Sometimes it makes me think that there is truth in reincarnation. Maybe you are being punished for something you have done in your previous life." She was in tears while she was talking to me.

I have the best family in the world. Everyone is so wonderful, loving and kind. When one needed help everybody would help without being asked. Greed is one negative virtue that is unknown among my siblings and that is the legacy of our most loving, gentle, kind, compassionate and generous father. Everyone is so caring and ready to help whoever is in need. My brother Boyet one time popped up in my apartment and said, "Come, I'll take you to a movie." He knew my husband had left me and so he was there to take me to the movies. Of all the movies to go to, he chose to see The Champ introducing a little child actor who did a good job making me cry. I did not bother to carry my purse with me, and I did not have any handkerchief, so I used my dress collar to wipe my tears. The movie was such a tearjerker. My brother Reg who had a flourishing Electrical Engineering professional practice promised to support my children's expenses while I was gone.

CHAPTER 9

America, Here I Come!

I don't really want to think of that moment I left my country for the first time because it was the saddest moment of my life to leave my children and all my loved ones behind, not knowing how long I would be away. One very nice flight attendant tried to comfort me because I was crying during the entire duration of the flight. I arrived at Fort Lauderdale on June 1, 1980. Anita and Paul were at the airport waiting for me. Paul was very impressed that I had just landed in America and yet I was speaking English the way I did. I was very happy to see them. Anita was on her eight months of pregnancy. She looked so big in her middle.

Back in the eighties, Fort Lauderdale was not exactly what I imagined the United States would be because it sort of look like a dumpy place and the sights I saw were disappointing. I then realized that only pictures of the most impressive US sceneries are the ones that appear on magazines that are exported abroad, but anyway, going to the US was what I needed to heal the wound in my heart caused by my broken marriage. The new environment, the excitement of an American adventure made me forget the entire emotional burden that I was carrying.

Years went by so fast. I ended up becoming a permanent resident of the United States and my children came to join me in 1983 but I was back in the Philippines to be with them during the last four months of 1982, so I was not away from them for the whole three years and we had constant telephone conversations along the way. I remember my little Tentong saying, "Mama, it seems like I have not seen you for a very long long long time," after being away from them for over a year and it broke my heart but that was all over now. It was a very joyous moment for me when my young ones finally came to join me in May of 1983. I watched them grow and each year that passed, my fear that my broken marriage would have adverse effect on my children's emotional development became less and less. They were the best children any mother can have. They were constantly in the honor roll. Every time I attended a parent-teacher meeting, their teachers would always complement me for having well-behaved children and they all told me that it was a pleasure for them to be the teacher of my children. My children never gave me problems related to drugs or alcohol, or reckless sex whatsoever and they all grew up to become good wholesome law-abiding citizens whom I am so proud of. If I knew this would be the outcome, I would not have worried as much when they were little.

My children and I were always a team when they were growing up. They all wanted me to be with them, even going to movies they would like to see unlike other teenagers who would be embarrassed to be seen with their parents when they are with their friends. During Football season, all the high school kids would hangout at Pizza Hut after the games and I would be with them. One time at Pizza Hut, while we were seated on a booth waiting for our orders, a pretty teenage girl came and sat next to Tentong and started flirting with him unabashed completely unaware that Tentong's Mom was across the table watching. Most people thought I looked young for my age, so she probably did not realize right away that I was the mother of the boy she was flirting with, but when she gazed at Raqui and then at me who was looking at her with apparent amusement she probably realized that I was not Tentong's sister and therefore I was his Mom. She immediately jumped to her feet and ran to the bathroom, and she let out a big scream of embarrassment inside what she thought was the privacy of the bathroom, but I could hear her screaming from where we sat. I thought it was so funny.

We carried on playing the games that we started to play together when they were still very young like the game of hearts. After work, I would cook dinner and we would play games after dinner. Soon some of their friends in the neighborhood came to join us in our games and before long my home became the gathering place of all my children's friends who played with us. Charades became one of our favorites. After playing it for a few times we decided that Raqui and Tentong should not be teammates because they seem to have mental telepathy, they knew exactly what was on each other's mind and they were unbeatable when they teamed up in charades. Trivial Pursuit and Pictionary were also among our favorites. My light beige carpet quickly turned brown because of the heavy traffic of Yayoy's, Raqui's and Tentong's friends coming every night to play with us but I did not mind. Some mothers did not want other kids messing up their home, but I was happy that my kids were at my home with their friends doing wholesome fun activities with me.

I was very happy that my profession enabled me to earn enough money to support all my children through college. If Mama did not persuade me to aspire to be an Architect instead of an art painter, I don't know if I could have done this. Being highly capable in a male dominated profession enabled me to earn as much as the guys if not more. To my surprise, I did not meet any one in the United states whom I worked with, who had abilities comparable to mine. I did pen and ink renderings of perspective drawings of proposed structures for marketing brochures, I made expertly executed scaled models of luxury homes, I did energy calculations for Airconditioning systems, and I can read surveyor's technical description of a parcel of land, and these are some of my capabilities my other workmates did not possess. Architectural designing and preparation of construction documents are required abilities of all Architect. At Ames Design International, where I was employed before the advent of computerized drafting, Peter, the plan checker, consulted me for mathematical calculations of dimensions requiring trigonometry. He called me the math wiz bang. I am also a builder, the luxury home that I was in charge of construction, aside from being the Architect on site, got the Construction the Year Award at the City it was built.

My two boys graduated from college without any student loan, as far as I know. They might have availed themselves of student loans without telling me but I know I paid for their tuitions, board and lodgings. I had a joint bank account with each of them and that's how I sent them money. Raqui committed herself to a student loan to enroll at a college for a Fashion Merchandising course when she declined my offer to send her to a nursing school. I am also very grateful to my employers for being so trusting and understanding that they allowed me to take my work home to be able to work extra hours at night so that I can make extra money needed to afford the extra curricular activities expenses of the children. There were music lessons for all three of them, band camp for Tentong who was an active member of the high school band, Drill team camp for Raqui, who was the captain of the Drill team marching with the high school band, aside from her fashion modeling lessons, and college tuition and school supplies and dormitory expenses for Yayoy who was so smart he was in college at UF at age sixteen. Yayoy took the high school entrance exam and qualified to be freshman at age 12, he was constantly on the Dean's list at UF and he was a UF Piano Concerto Competition winner while he was an Electrical Engineering student. There were times when I would ask to be excused from our after dinner games because I had worked to do but Tentong would say, "But Ma, it's not the same if you're not playing with us," so we would chose to play games like Trivial Pursuit so that I could be busy working on my drafting board right next to them while I was waiting for my turn to play.

When they got to high school, my work evolved from manual drafting to computerized drafting and all the children wanted to help me produce the architectural drawings in the computer. It was a novelty, and they were all enthusiastic to produce the drawings with the help of the computer using the CAD program so our group games evolved into doing CAD operations to produce Architectural plans plus I paid them a generous amount of $100 for every sheet of drawing that they produced. One thing about computerized drawings is that no one can tell who the operator was unlike drawings by hand, which are like a handwriting, and you can tell one handwriting from another. I carefully red marked the corrections on the drawings that the children produced until they attain the quality of the kind of drawings I would produce so that my employer, who were not aware that my children were helping me with my work, would not complain or think that the quality of my work degenerated.

It was Yayoy who got me into learning how to CAD. He is so smart that he learned to CAD by just reading the book at a time when computer operations were purely by DOS. Raqui and Tentong learned to CAD easily too because these young generation grew up with computerized gadgets. Yayoy talked me into investing in a computer so that they can all do CAD, acronym for computer-aided drafting. Soon we had two computer stations because all of them wanted to CAD at the same time during summer when they were out of school. Still the two computer stations were not enough for all four of them, a friend included, to CAD so we had day shifts and the night shifts. When the CAD program was new, the plotting service was so expensive, it cost more than fifty dollar per page to produce the hard copy of the drawings and CAD was useless if the drawings were not plotted so I had to buy a pen plotter that cost me more than four thousand dollars, which soon was obsolete when ink jet plotters came in the market. This all happened while Yayoy was still in high school.

When Yayoy left for college he left me with unfinished CAD projects, and I was forced to learn the program so that I could finish the project myself. So, I learned how to CAD out of necessity. I was constantly bothering Yayoy by phone while he was away in his college dorm and I was constantly asking for instructions when I got lost CADing and he would always tell me, "Ma, read the book!" Read the book? I was not born in the computer generation; how can I understand computer language? I somehow managed to learn CAD operation and I managed to make the transition from manual drafting to computerized drafting. The excitement of Raqui and Tentong for the novelty of the CAD program ebbed in no time and doing CAD became so boring for them so they were not of help for me when I was left with unfinished CAD jobs when Yayoy left for college. Raqui would rather work in the consignment shops at a nearby community park renting out sporting equipments during weekends. After school, Tentong who is more sociable than his siblings would rather be with friends working as helpers at the dining facility of an adult community, which was within walking distance from our condominium.

Our first home was a brand-new condominium unit built by my employer, MAP Builders, a very successful developer that built beautiful homes in the City where we lived. Junn came to the U.S. too around 1984 but I did not bother to demand any support from him for the children. He is now married to Virgie, a U.S. citizen Filipina and their marriage seems to be working but they don't have children so maybe that is the key or maybe Junn is now too old to carry on his philandering ways. I hope he is happy. He should have offered to help support the children, but he did not, and I knew that demanding child support from him would only cause me more emotional aggravations and I did not want any of that. As long as I can manage, we were alright. My children and I were happy campers. One Filipino told me that it would have been easier for me if my children had stayed in the Philippines, and I would have just sent them the dollars for support because the dollar is worth a lot more in the Philippines. "What are you talking about," I told her, "I was so miserable when I was away from them for over two years. I would have gone back home if they could not be with me when they did."

I was very happy that my children somehow grew up without any emotional hang-ups and none of them succumbed to any peer pressure that would have caused problems for me. They were all aware of our financial limitations and they never demanded anything that we could not afford. Raqui learned to sew her own clothes while she was in high school, and she believed me when I told her that clothes that we designed ourselves were worth more than any ready-made designer clothes in the stores because the clothes that we sew ourselves were custom made for us and custom made clothes are more expensive than ready to wear clothes on the market. So, she grew up unmindful that she was not wearing expensive designer's outfits. She was proud of the clothes that she wore to school, which she made herself. She wore the prettiest party dresses on prom nights, which I designed and sewed myself. Some mothers asked me if I could sew prom dresses for their daughters and I had to tell them that it might cost them more than what they can buy in stores because they would have to pay me by the hour at the same rate I was getting paid in my Architectural work. The Architectural office that employed me did not give me any limit on how many hours I would like to work each week. The more hours I put in each week, the happier my boss was. Construction in Florida in the eighties and nineties was booming at the time I was raising three children through college, perfect timing!

Soon Raqui was off to college too and she also started working. I was glad that she did not go to a college five hours drive away like Yayoy did. She was studying and working also. I hardly saw her because she came home just in time to go to bed. She became a manager of a fashion merchandizing outlet, but I saw the very dangerous responsibilities imposed on my very young Raqui. The store closed at 9:00 PM but by the time she was done with all activities required, it was almost midnight before she could deposit all sales money to the bank. I was happy when my sister Anita employed her as her secretary when she became the Administrator of a Dialysis clinic.

I was so heartbroken when Yayoy left for UF, I was crying two weeks before he left. When Tentong left to go to the same university, UF, where Yayoy was, I was completely broken down. I went into a severe depression. I suffered a severe empty nest syndrome. My children gave me the purpose to live and when they started having lives of their own, I felt like I was back to square one. There was no purpose for my life again. When I was a teenager, searching for a purpose for my life was a big crisis for me. My little book, The Imitation of Christ, made my search for a purpose harder because the book taught me to put myself last, so it was meaningless to aspire for something for myself. It was meaningless to pursue a career.

Junn gave me a purpose to live, especially when I realized he was sick and when his health was restored it was my three children that gave me the purpose for my life. When my role as a parent was over, I was lost again, and I went into severe depression. While I was suffering from empty nest syndrome, I lost my beloved Apang who died from complications of a stroke and that further sank me deeper into my depression. I had to start searching again for a purpose for my life to snap out of my severe depression and that was when Mother Nature came to the rescue. I have always loved nature, but I was too distracted by my children to fully savor the pleasure that nature brings. It was when I was alone that I experienced what the poets felt when they wrote beautiful poems about nature, I realized that my heart can really dance with the daffodils. I knew God was making me feel his love through nature. There was overflowing joy in my heart just to behold a beautiful flower, or the beautiful foliage of a tree dancing with the wind, a bird flying against a beautiful blue sky or a beautiful cloud formation. There was joy just beholding the countenance of an innocent child and much more so when I heard their joyful laughter. There was joy just watching a cute little squirrel and its graceful fluffy tail as it quickly climbs up a tree. There was joy watching my neighbors walking their pets around the block. Everything looked so beautiful, and I started to ask myself why I should fell forlorn when there is so much beauty to behold that can fill my heart with joy. Then I realized that I was sad because of my own selfishness, I was sad because I wanted my children to be close by my side all the time. It was my selfishness that was causing my sadness. I should rejoice that I succeeded bringing up my children on my own. I should rejoice that despite a broken marriage, my children had grown up to become successful citizens of this world. I then realized that I have found Eden. I was in Paradise.

I met a lady named Kathy who became a good friend at the time when my children were away in school. She was a skier. She taught me to roller blade in preparation for a training to learn to ski. We joined a ski group. I learned to ski, and it was so much fun. I was like being a child again gliding down the slopes at Snow Mass at Aspen, or Steamboat Spring in Colorado, or in Heavenly Tahoe and many other ski resorts. I tried the blue slopes, but they were too steep for me, I kept falling. I was happy enough at the green slopes. When it was not ski season, I played tennis with Kathy and her friends. She decided to move to Ohio and I miss her.

CHAPTER 10

I Traveled to All Seven Continents of Earth

I wrote the story of how my life in the U. S. started and how I ended up a naturalized citizen of the United States on my first book, The Book of life, after a God experience that revealed to me all the falsehoods of all organized religions. It is now forty-four years since I left the Philippines to become a permanent resident in the United States. During these past two decade I was able to travel to different nations around the world in fact, I have set foot on all seven continents of planet Earth. At the time I was in Hong Kong, it happened to be the day-off of all domestic helps in Hong Kong and they were all out on the streets picnicking, thousands of them seated on the street pavements and they were all Filipino domestic helpers. They brought their food, and they were all having meals while seated right on the asphalted streets of Hong Kong which were closed for traffic to give them space to hang out. Some were strumming their guitars singing their favorite melodies while the others were busily chatting with their friends. I could not understand what was going on at first. I knew they were Filipinos because I could understand their language. I was wondering if they were waiting for some sort of a pop concert.

I asked one of them why they were all gathered out on the street, "Mayroon ba kayong hinihintay?" (Are you waiting for something?)

"Wala po 'mam', day-off po namin. Nagrerelax lang po kami," the lady seated on the pavement answered.

"Bakit hindi kayo magpicnic sa Park? Bakit nandito kayo sa kalye?" I asked further. (Why don't you picnic at the park? Why are you on the streets?) The lady just looked at me in a way that told me without saying a word, "Why are you asking such a question?" I went on my way not too far off, I found myself at a Hong Kong Park, and I saw the reason why the Filipino domestic helpers were picnicking on the streets. The Park was reserved for their masters who were leisurely walking, enjoying the spaciousness of the park all to themselves, some walking their dogs. Some doing their limbering exercise Tai Chi or reading a book peacefully on a bench. I can't stop feeling sorry for my fellow kababayan who apparently were not free to enjoy the spacious beautifully landscaped park where they can relax on their day off. Why did they prefer to come to Hong Kong to be treated like second class citizens? Was this a better quality of life for them?

Anywhere I go around the world I do my sightseeing walking because I love to walk and because I get to know these strange places more by walking. I meet Filipinos while walking on the streets of these foreign lands. Somehow, I can tell from the way they look and from their demeanor that they are Filipinos and much more when I hear them conversing with each other because I recognize their language. I greet them and after exchanging pleasantries, I find out that they are domestic helps. The Philippines seems to be the supplier of domestic helps of the world. Filipino professionals in foreign countries probably drive cars so I don't meet them walking on the streets. I bet most of these domestic helpers send whatever they are earning back to the Philippines to support their loved ones, so they are not able to accumulate assets for themselves. The Philippine government is very happy with this arrangement because of the dollars that are sent home by the overseas workers. On a Cruise ship, it is very common to find dining rooms and kitchens staffed by Filipino workers.

Now that I have seen several countries on all the continents of Earth, I can't stop admiring Europeans and Asians because of their apparent love for their own cultures which they regard with great pride and respect, and I wonder why I don't see this trait among Filipinos. What I see in the Philippines is that everyone wants to imitate the Western people particularly the Americans. I have visited the Philippines several times since I left in 1980 and I have observed many things that disappointed me. Why do I feel ashamed when I hear Filipinos delivering their speeches in the Philippines in the English language? Everywhere else in the world people are so proud of their native language. I happened to be in the Philippines to watch a College Basketball championship game and the leader of the winning team who accepted the honors gave speeches in English and I ask myself why can't he talk in Tagalog? It is very common for Filipino Government officials to address Filipinos on Television in English. If anyone would want to know why I am writing in the English language, the reason is that I have a message in this book intended for all of humanity in our world. I can write in Tagalog if I want to, I know it will be harder for me now that I have lived in a foreign land for more than half of my life, but I know I can still do it. But how about those who lived in the Philippines all their lives? Why do they address their kababayan in English?

I was dismayed when I saw what the Filipinos did to Quiapo Church. Every where in the world people do everything to preserve antiquities with historical values but not the Filipinos. I remember what a beautiful piece of Filipino-Spanish Baroque Architecture Quiapo Church was, and they destroyed it. Isn't there a Historic preservation Agency in the Philippines? Doesn't the Secretary of Tourism of the Philippines know that antiquities and historical relics appeal to tourists? They did the same thing to Antipolo Church. I remember that one of my last house inspection duties that I performed while I was an Appraiser was of some houses in Antipolo and I visited the Church before I went home. I was so dismayed when I saw it again when I visited the Philippines. Whoever thought that what they are doing to these historic Architectural buildings are improvements are awfully mistaken because antiquity is priceless and now that they are destroyed, they can never be replaced and if they think that what they have done is beautiful then I say their aesthetic sense is very much still lacking. It was a crime what they did to the Jose Rizal Shrine. I remember my visit to the National Heroes Shrine when I was a pupil at Pio Del Pilar Elementary School. I really felt the ambiance of how Rizal, whom I admire so much spent the last moments of his life and it was a beautiful experience that I still feel today when I recall those moments of my visit to his shrine. Young Filipinos of today are robbed of the memorable experience I had as a child because the Shrine has been destroyed. The Luneta Park, the site of the martyrdom of Rizal is now unrecognizable because Filipino values are misplaced. They value more the artificial peace of real estate that destroyed the beautiful site where one can watch the glorious sun set at Manila Bay while at the same time gracing the historic site of the monument to the martyrdom of the great hero, Jose Rizal.

The last time I visited Iriga, I asked my cousin Purita who lives there, "Whatever happened to Burabod?" She told me that it is no longer the way it used to be. It is now fenced-in in the midst of a congested housing site and some people don't even know that it ever existed. I hope people around it are not dumping their raw sewage into that once upon a time a beautiful enchanted freshwater pond, the very image of paradise that I used to know, just like the way people are dumping their raw sewage on every river in the Philippines including the one that feeds the water falls at Hinulugang Taktak. One of the reasons of the poverty of this Country of my birth is that the people have no appreciation for the beautiful endowments of mother nature. In all other nations that I have visited, the government protects the natural beauty of spectacular sites and turns them into parks where people can relax and enjoy the wondrous sights. The Burabod could have been turned into a beautiful tourist attraction that could bring in revenue for the City of Iriga but they chose to waste Mother Nature's gift. The Pasig river is so dirty and polluted like every other river in the nation because the people see it primarily as a place to dump their wastes and they don't think in terms of looking at these rivers as Mother Natures endowments to beautify the land. I know that one of the reasons for this is a corrupt government run by corrupt officials who steal the money intended to improve infrastructures that would provide proper wastes disposals and sewage treatment plants to its people.

A corrupt administration erected a monument to honor the return of General Douglas McArthur during the Second World War to reclaim the Philippine Islands from the Japanese. I heard someone, who came from the province where the monument was erected, complained that this monument was destroyed by a vengeful succeeding administration. The people's money had already been spent on something that could be useful as a tourist attraction. What benefit did the unnecessary destruction of the monument give to the people of the nation whose tax money was spent on it already? The disheartened complainant believes that the only reason for its destruction was to satisfy the vengeance of an incompetent president who was too preoccupied by trivialities in stead of focusing on important matters such as implementing measures that would safe guard the source of the water supply of Metro Manila which became infected by disease-causing bacteria, and many died of Typhoid in this modern day and age.

I have seen country sides all over the world and it seems to me that it is only in the Philippines where I see idle farmlands. All farmlands that I saw all over the United States, in European countries like Italy, France, England, Spain, Switzerland, or in Asian countries like China, Thailand or Vietnam, were all producing something. I did not see any wasted farmland anywhere else in the world that I have visited except in the Philippines. China is mostly mountainous terrain, but they till the mountain sides to produce crops for food or terraced it to produce rice and this is what I saw all along the river side while cruising the Yangtze. I saw how industrious the Vietnamese people are and how proud they are of their heritage. It is heartbreaking for me to hear that the Philippines cannot even produce enough rice for its own consumption, she has to import from Vietnam. Why do young Filipinos prefer to be second class citizens in foreign countries as domestic helpers rather than till the land as farmers? It is a common aspiration for young Filipinos to get education that will give them a chance to immigrate abroad but why? I left the country of my birth with a heavy heart. As a young woman I never aspired to leave the country of my birth. Most of my classmates in college sought for chances to immigrate to the United States as soon as we graduated but I did not. It was not through my own volition that I left the Philippines but even if I did leave my country, my love for my native land had never diminished one bit and deep in my heart the longing to go back home had never ceased. I know I will spend the last days of my life back in my native land.

I saw Western movies depicting the corruptions in the Philippines. I saw Western movies showing young Filipina girls kidnapped and sold as sex slaves while Filipino policemen who were supposed to protect the poor helpless victims were bribed handsomely to look the other way and allowed the perpetrations of such heinous crimes and I know that these stories are based on facts because I spent three months of staying in the Philippines to help women who were victims of human trafficking, to help them get back on their feet after a despicable ordeal. I help in a sort of work therapy to help them regain their dignity. I taught these victims how to crochet. I supplied them with crochet hooks and thread. I saw a documentary about them being recruited as stage performers, singers or domestic help but they ended up as sex slaves against their will, prisoners of the recruiters who held their passports so that they couldn't do anything. These evil recruiters are surely on their way to burn on the lake of fire!

I have encountered an American Company that produces water proofing products looking for production sites in Asia and I offered the land that my mother owns as an ideal site because it is in Naga City in Bicol and I was thinking it would create work opportunities for Bicolanos plus it would give the Filipinos the chance to learn their new water proofing technology but the owners of the Company would never go to the Philippines because of the government corruptions and rampant crimes that they hear about. They knew all the Philippine government officials would demand bribes before they could get their business started aside from taking the risk of being kidnapped for ransom if they would step in Philippine soil. They established their production operation in Malaysia.

This is obviously the legacy of Western Colonization of the Philippines. Filipinos are individualistic people and only their own personal or immediate family interest matters to them. They don't think in terms of what is good for the whole country. They elect government officials who would give them personal benefits without considering what this official can do to improve the nation as a whole and worse they elect incompetent officials just because they are their movie idols. Western culture is materialistic. Filipinos are indoctrinated in schools formulated with Western values that measures success in terms of material possessions. Poor Filipinos would rather be domestic helpers abroad because they get instant material gratification in the form of the almighty dollar. Filipinos do not respect manual labor so people who do manual work get paid very low wages so they go abroad so that their labor would be paid in dollars even if it is Hong Kong dollars the equivalent in pesos is still higher.

The ultimate result of capitalism in the United States is beginning to be felt by Americans. American middle class is dwindling while the number of people on the poverty level is rising. The few ultra rich multinationals whose main motivation is greed has closed their manufacturing establishments in the United States and they are all now in China where the labor cost is still very low because the Chinese government has no labor laws that protects exploitation of Chinese laborers, and all the profits are amassed by these few mega rich multi-national corporations who are the only ones benefiting in the globalization of industries. I see them as the resurrection of the Monarchy of the past with a different name, instead of Kings and Queens, and Royalties they are the Corporate magnates and the CEOs. History repeats itself. We have seen in the past that Nations populated mostly with suffering poor people ruled by the few mega rich ruling class who wallow in extreme luxury uncaring of the sufferings of the poor and are too greedy to share their wealth to improve the quality of life of the rest of the population collapsed due to a violent clamor for change by the suffering majority. European countries must have learned from their past that their democratic way of government has implemented measures to maintain a high standard of living for their people. They have an effective way of dispersing wealth to all, good public services such as efficient transportation system, medical benefits and they are able to maintain their middle class. On the other hand, the United States is losing their middle class, and the government must do something to avert a catastrophe.

The Americans continue to clamor for higher wages and the higher their minimum wages get the more they lose the chance to compete with production cost of other Nations with lower labor cost such as China. One of the effects of raising minimum wages is the higher cost of commodities. The American dollar continues to devaluate while the value of the Euros is getting higher. Americans are losing their jobs while the economy of China is booming. China on the other hand is becoming more polluted because the Chinese government's priority is the economy and they do not care if their people are dying because of the pollution. Are they prioritizing the economy over the health of the people because they are the most populous country on earth anyway? How sad.

Manufacturing in the United States is nearing its complete demise because to amass more profits American Corporations keep on outsourcing jobs that require manpower to third world countries that have much lower labor cost. These greedy Corporate Magnates doesn't care if Americans are losing their jobs and all they care for is to amass all the wealth in the world which in turn bring them all the power to safeguard their wealth. So, the only jobs available are service jobs. Construction workers and farm workers are in demand, so millions of

Mexicans cross the borders illegally to earn the almighty dollars. These illegal aliens have no problems getting employed because they are willing to work for much less wages than Americans who are used to higher standards of living.

Someone came up with statistics showing that in the U.S. the fastest ethnic population growth, is that of Hispanics and at the rate they are growing, in time, they will be the majority ethnic group in the United States and the American friend who told me about this was so alarmed. I told him, "The way I look at it, these Hispanics are called Hispanics because they are Spanish speaking people but ethnically, they are the descendants of the Native American Indians who are now reclaiming their land." What goes around comes around. The Europeans drove the native inhabitants of the Americas out of their land now their descendants are coming back to reclaim their land through birth and immigration, legal or not, and no one can stop them.

Nurses are always in demand so many Filipinos aspire to become nurses to get to the U.S., but nurses are mostly women, what kind of work would their spouse find aside from being a laborer? I see many highly educated Filipinos working as waiters in restaurants and they avoid eye contact with me, and they are evasive to start any conversation because of the Filipino trait of being ashamed of doing a laborer's job. They should not feel that way because labor is respected in the U. S. Technical jobs have already been transported to other countries with lower labor cost such as India. Every time I need technical support whether banking related or computer problem related, the 888 number that I call for assistance is always answered by an operator with a heavy Indian accent. One time, out of curiosity, I asked if the operator was stationed in India and I got a yes answer.

I see no more reason why Filipinos should still aspire to go to the United States or to any other foreign land now that globalization has come but what should be done so that Filipinos would aspire to make the Philippines an ideal place to live in instead of trying to improve one's quality of life by going to another country. I am convinced that the Western way, the materialistic way, which is Capitalism, is not the way to Utopia because cravings for material things are never quenched and the more you get material things the more you want, and it never ends. Unfortunately, the whole of humanity has adopted the Western way and looks up to those who had amassed wealth as their hero and aspire to become rich too but those who are already on top had amassed power along with their wealth and they will do everything they can to gain absolute power over everyone else and they eradicate upcoming smaller enterprises that pose as a threat to their empires by buying them out or by whatever means. There are others who express their disdain for the Western way through violence in the name of religion, which is threatening the very existence of the whole of humanity.

Right now, there is a big cry for Socialism in the US. Is humanity really ready for socialism? The Soviet Union collapsed because many lost the endeavor to better themselves when they lost the need to compete with their peers to survive. Many resorted to alcoholism (because of boredom?) when the challenge of competition was taken away. There are also those who take advantage and just demand handouts doing nothing. A couple of years ago, a big throng of protestors were destroying major cities in the US, painting all sort of graffities that are abominable eyesores, destroying monuments of the past to erase the evidence of the continuing evolution of man on earth. They made a big display of destruction and not improvement. What caused this? Homo Sapiens may have reached the pinnacle of physiological evolution but it is still in the process of intellectual and emotional evolution and these protestors must be enlightened of this fact to stop their ignorance that is causing these despicable unlawfulness and destruction of this beautiful country. They burn their own flag. What comes to mind when you see a flag of a nation? The flag is a symbol of your country, your fatherland. Is it just to disrespect and hurt your father for the misdeeds of your brothers? Burning your own flag is treason! If you hate this country, leave, go to a country that you can love. No one is forcing you to stay here. I doubt if you can find one better than the United States of America.

I say that I have found my paradise here on earth because I have attained complete peace within myself and I also learned to accept my position as a mere insignificant observer of all these disturbing things that are going on in our world, but I have not lost hope for humanity because I know that behind every cloud, the sun still shines. For as long as there is life there is hope. I am writing my book because it is the only thing I can do. Whether my book can contribute something to humanity or nothing at all, I do not know, and I will never know if I do not do it so I might as well try. I have learned to find joy from the simplest things in life that are free like a beautiful flower, a gorgeous landscape, seascape or sunset, a beautiful sky, cute little animals, and so much more from laughter of little children, my grandchildren are my bundles of joy and my own children, and my family are my best friends as well as other people who are so dear to me. This came to me when I learned to free myself from want. The more I learned from life the more I find the profoundness of the words of Jesus.

When Jesus said, "Give up all you material possessions, come and follow me," I learned that what he meant was stop wanting everything to go your way or wanting material things and you will find your inner peace and when you find your inner peace you will find true happiness. He did not mean give up all material things and become a beggar and a burden to society because by being so you lose your dignity and without dignity you cannot find inner peace. When my Raqui graduated from college, I gathered all the jewelry that I accumulated through the years, put it in a box, and gave it to her as graduation present. It wasn't much but Raqui was wide eyed and dumbfounded when she opened her present, all she could say was a long-surprised Ma! I told her, I don't need them anymore. Suddenly, I understood what Jesus said, I felt sooo free! I have freed myself from material want! Hallelujah!

CHAPTER 11

Finally, I Found Paradise Right Here on Earth!

B elieve it or not, one can really find Paradise right here on planet earth and I realized that it is true that when you are in Paradise, you can hear God. I heard the voice of God, the Supreme Power Above and that was when I realized what the true purpose of life is. This is the main reason why I wrote this book. My story is a testimony of my honesty. Every person I wrote about is real and they can all testify to my honesty. I would go through a lie detector test, or you may subject me to a truth serum if needed to prove the truthfulness of my story. I left my native land not through my own volition, but now I realized that it was fate that sent me to a foreign land to attain a better understanding of our world, which was necessary to understand the language of God.

My beloved Mama passed away peacefully on May 2, 2010, I flew home to be with my beloved siblings at her funeral. I heartfully sang the Lord's Prayer for my beloved Mother at her memorial service and I made a photo collage in celebration of her life. A couple of years later, I told my sister Mila that she must have reincarnated already. I had a big suspicion that she reincarnated as my beautiful grandniece whom I met for the first time when she was just a year old. I was a stranger to her but on my first visit to meet her, she climbed up on my knee and was so lovey-dovey to me, rubbing her nose to mine. How could a little one year old give me such a wonderful affectionate greeting when I was a stranger to her?

I told Mila that my beliefs now did not come from any man but directly from God. The only way we can reach heaven is to rapture body and soul to be one with God, but she cannot believe that only Jesus is in heaven because she is thinking only of the inhabitants of earth. I told her that her question is already answered by John 3;13, which only pertains to our planet earth though. Jesus said I am not of this kingdom; did he mean he came from a more advance planet? Was he a highly evolved alien capable of making the lame walk, the blind to see and bring the dead back to life, who incubated in the womb of a virgin on a mission for God to lead us to eternal life? Our planet earth is a minute speck in all of creation. How many more inhabited planets are there in this vast universe? It is a pure misconception that heaven is inhabited by humanoid spirits. Heaven is what the Buddhists call the power of the universe. God is the power of the universe. When you go to heaven you become one with God because you join the power of the Universe which is pure energy devoid of form. God, heaven and the power of the Universe is one and the same pure sentient energy. To think that the power of the Universe cannot think on its own as what some Guru says is falsehood because it communicated with me and told me all these messages that I am imparting to you. I am sure that God laid down the laws of life or His Commandments unto Moses in the same manner as God had revealed all these truths to me that I am hereby imparting to you.

The process of transformation of our whole being into energy is actually an anti matter process because matter is turned back to energy, but it is sentient energy because it is energy derived from an intelligent entity. I know many will find this concept too radical but that is what I was told. Another way matter is transformed into pure energy is through the black hole but the energy that will be produced will not be sentient and the ultimate purpose of life is to produce sentient energy. We, intelligent beings are given free will. If you are not ready to join the power of the universe then live an earthly life and you will stay on earth for as long as you like being born again and again in a perpetual cycle but follow the guidelines set forth by God otherwise your life will come to its permanent demise, and no more rebirths for you because your life program will be terminated, deleted, extinguished permanently.

God also showed me Daniel 2:22, a passage on the scriptures that also has the sign the end times, the pattern of 2, which says, "*He reveals deep and secret things, he knows what is in the darkness and the light dwells with him.*" Indeed, deep and secret things were revealed to me, which I could never have conceived of on my own, and I would never have come to know them if God did not reveal them to me. I did not know that these passages in the Bible existed, I was not a Bible reader, I bought a Bible out of curiosity, but God showed them to me in a mysterious way. God bade me to read the scriptures and the Bible when I held it in my hands, mysteriously opened unto the pages where the passages that God wanted me to read were written and my eyes gazed exactly upon the words God meant for me to read and the text of these words on the scriptures floated into mid-air as they were magnified a hundred fold while I saw visions explaining its meaning to me. The sensation I felt was that of hearing rather than reading and I felt the presence of God encompassing my whole being and this is, believe it or not, the whole truth and God is my witness.

Another sign is that Jesus was a carpenter and a carpenter gets involved in building houses whereas I am an Architect who had build houses too. God sent me, a woman, to be his messenger for our generation to show us that man and woman are equal in the eyes of God. Jesus specifically said that "*For **she** shall come from the uttermost part of the earth,*" and surely the land of my birth is the most uttermost part of the earth at the time Jesus spoke these words two thousand years ago.

What ever indoctrination you have in the past are all part of salvation plan, but it is now time to hear the new message that God wants us to follow to reach our ultimate destination. Jesus said, "*I came not to bring peace but a sword*," because he had foreseen that mankind is not evolved enough to understand the true meaning of his words and indeed, unto this day, mankind still resort to bloodshed to settle disputes. For our generation, the sword of Jesus is to sever the old from the new. It is time to discern false doctrines of a man-made gods from the true words of the true God. Bible fundamentalists believe that they know exactly how God would come again but Jesus said no one knows but the Father so why believe anyone who claims that they know. I am giving you the true meaning of the Bible directly from the true God. Believe me I did not have any prior clue what the message would be before God spoke to me.

I did not know the Bible at all. I grew up in the Philippines at the time when Catholic priests discouraged Bible readings but I am telling you now that the Catholic Church, in spite of all their flaws, did the right thing to me by preaching only the words of Jesus. If I had been brain washed by man made interpretations of Bible fundamentalists who preach that the whole Bible is the word of the true God, I would not have recognized that it was the true God speaking to me. If I knew I would be given this task I would have lived my life differently so don't judge me because Moses had killed a man and yet, God chose him to give us the Commandments. What I know of the Bible came to me miraculously directly from God. I am a witness for Jesus and for the Commandments of God that was written in stone through the hand of Moses. I know that all Abrahamic religions will be gnashing their teeth when I reveal all the secrets of all Abrahamic religion scriptures that was revealed to me by God. I am living proof that God exists, and I reiterate what Jesus said, "*Repent you sinners for the kingdom of heaven is at hand*."

I shared this revelation to a discussion forum sponsored by the Public Broadcasting System on the Internet and one Bible fundamentalist called me a blasphemer because all Bible fundamentalists believe that everything that is written in the Bible came from the true God, but not so, God told me. This is one of the reasons why Jesus rebuked the scribes of the Old Testament. I was subjected to all sorts of insults at this PBS discussion forum when I tried to share with them everything that was revealed to me by the true God. A Bible fundamentalist said that I exalted myself and I should be debased but God assured me, through the words of Jesus, that my lamp is lit so I must raise it up so that others may be enlightened as well. I thank a gentleman name Joshua Israel who backed me up and stood beside me during the entire proceedings of the discussion. Joshua's support made all the insults bearable.

I cannot show any sensitivity to beliefs that are contrary to what I am revealing because there is only one God, and it is Him who sent me to reveal the truth. Jesus was crucified because his dogma threatened the established religious hierarchy of his time, after all he said, "*You don't need to go to the synagogue to pray, pray in secret*". I expect this to happen to my mission as well. All religious leaders demand respect for their faith which are laden with man-made dogma and false beliefs, but my mission is from the true God and I must obey for the sake of humanity. Jesus said, "*If salt has lost its savor, it is not good for anything but to be trampled upon.*" Differences in religious belief systems are the root of our present world problems, hatred towards non-believers of their faith even resulting in deadly confrontations and wars. Religion is supposed to bring peace on earth, but the violence perpetrated in the name of religion is making peace on earth unattainable. God wants us to do away with our present religions and we should only believe one true pure faith so that we could finally find the long-awaited peace on earth. I, whose name is Pure in universal language, is sent by God so that the new belief system will now be just Pure faith, free of man-made false beliefs. This is the judgment of God that I was sent to announce to humanity. God showed me that the four beasts mentioned in the Revelation are emblems of four world powers that propagated major belief systems to our world that are keeping mankind earthbound preventing our specie from attaining intellectual purity to evolve into a higher state of being. You will never reach heaven if you adhere to your current religion because all present religions on earth are tainted with false dogmas.

We are all connected to our creator like a computer network, so it is wrong to think that your thoughts are privately yours alone. All contributors to collective evil thoughts that manifested through a weak mortal and resulted in a crime are responsible for that crime regardless of whether the contributor to the evil energy did not physically participate in the act. Crimes mirror the fact that mankind entertains evil thoughts. We humans are given free will. We are free to do what we want to do with our lives, but Jesus clearly told us the consequences of our choices. God does not punish but there are laws of life that cannot be defied. If you choose the path of evil, Jesus told you that you would go hell but there is redemption even in hell if you choose to be redeemed because hell is right here on planet earth and if you think you are having a hellish life it is because you are in hell. If you don't show any remorse for your crimes, then you are surely bound to the finality of the lake of fire where there is no longer any chance for redemption after your life ends in the death of both your physical body and the death of your soul. The death of the soul is the second death mentioned in the Bible. The purpose of life is to reach perfection to attain immortality but if you chose a corrupted life then your life shall be terminated to burn in the lake of fire.

The soul of man, if translated into present terminology is a life program encoded in vibrating strings of energies that joins the fetus of a fertilized ovum during conception. This life program started from a very simple single celled microorganism and has evolved to become the life forms in our world today. God showed me through the words of Jesus on his parable about the seed and the sower that we indeed evolved from simple celled microorganism to become the intelligent beings that we are now. The vibrating strings of energies encoded with life programs were the seeds planted on our planet earth and God was the Sower. The intent of our life programs is to reach perfection until such time that we can join the power of the universe. God gave us the guidelines towards perfection, which are the Commandments handed down to us through Moses and if we choose to go against these guidelines our life programs shall be terminated and the remaining strings of energies that has lost its life program becomes subatomic particles in the magma on earth's mantle. The magma that comes out during volcanic eruptions is the lake of fire. This is what God showed me as the meaning of *to burn in hell fire* and *those whose name is not on the Book of life shall be cast unto the lake of fire*. If you are a habitual violator of the Commandments, your name shall be erased from the Book of Life.

No one wants to die because the will to live is inherent in human psyche because the primary objective of our life program is to live forever. Life expectancy is getting longer and longer because of advances in our knowledge of our physiology. Researches on longevity give us better understanding of genes that causes aging and death. Jesus said, "*If you believe in me you will not die.*" We all seek for long life because we are programmed to want to live forever except the followers of the false prophet. The false prophet had reprogrammed his followers to want to die. They are going against the intent of creation and their reprogramming is endangering our world because they believe that the destruction of our world is already cast in stone and they believe it is the will of God to end our world. Believe me, I was sent by God with the message that we have a chance to save our world if we successfully convince the followers of the false prophet that they have been deceived. This false prophet said that he was the last prophet that god would send on earth and he claimed that his message was god's final message because after him there would be no more prophets from god. I am living proof that he lied.

God showed me that the man-made god who demands human sacrifice, the same false god who tried to deceive Abraham into sacrificing his son, is still very much alive because with his disguise still unveiled he manifested to the false prophet and the demand for human sacrifice was disguised as dying for God. The False prophet planted the seed of hatred in the heart of the children of Ishmael to hate their brothers, the children of Isaac so that the demand for human sacrifice can be easily carried out and their father Abraham is so distraught. This false prophet successfully convinced his followers by claiming that Jesus foretold his coming as the next prophet of God, but the truth is that he was the false prophet that

Jesus warned mankind about, who would come in sheep's clothing but is a ravenous wolf whose aim is to send all the people on earth to their permanent death, body and soul. His god is the god of death, the true God is the God of the living.

We have witnessed countless of this human sacrifice, voluntarily marching to their death, taking innocent lives with them to please their god whose thirst for human blood is unquenchable. Their false god demand that all the children of Isaac be wiped out in the face of the earth and any nation who come to the aid of the children of Isaac will face their wrath. The dilemma in the Middle East has no solution for as long as the followers of the false prophet remain unenlightened of the truth that they are all worshipping a false god who demands human sacrifice who is very much pleased by their violent religious wars and murders of innocent victims. Vindictive Christians are not true followers of Jesus and they have fallen right into the trap of the god who demands human sacrifice who is none other than Satan and they too are marching to death as sacrifices, much to Satan's delight. There is no such a thing as holy war. The true God does not sanction any war because war violates His Commandment, "*Do not kill.*"

Jesus said, "*I did not come to destroy the law but to fulfill them.*" On the other hand, the dogma of this false prophet violates God's Commandments and these false commandments are hidden among dogmas borrowed from Jesus. Instilling hatred in the hearts of the deceived was so successful that they are even killing each other because they cannot agree on who is the rightful heir of the false prophet much to the delight of their false god. They take great pride of their murders, and they show the whole world their gruesome deeds of beheading their innocent victims on the Internet with great elation believing that all their gruesome deed has satisfied the thirst for human blood of their false god. Followers of the false prophet are forbidden to read the Gospels of Jesus, so they don't hear the warning of Jesus of the coming of the false prophet. The deceived followers of the false prophet are brain washed to voluntarily take their lives to kill those who refuse to follow their dogma. We have witnessed countless of these poor deceived souls who committed suicide to please their god who promised to reward them with eternal happiness in paradise with virgins who would satisfy the earthly cravings of their flesh. Paradise with virgins is an earthly reward for earthly desires that can only exist in a physical world. One who still has earthly desires cannot yet enter heaven. God is the God of the living and not of the dead. No dead can enter heaven. We can only get to paradise when we all learn to live peacefully with one another right here on planet earth. Those who turned themselves into human bombs to kill many others have gone straight to the lake of fire because they did not have any chance to repent for their grievous deed. May God have mercy on those who regard these suicide bombers as martyrs so that they may be enlightened of the truth otherwise they too, are headed for the lake of fire.

Those people who follow a belief system that urges them to commit suicide to kill others who refuse to conform to their beliefs have met the demise of their souls and they will not be born again, and their life is over, gone forever. The demise of the soul is the second death which is final. It is imperative that we save these poor misguided souls by enlightening them of the truth. God showed me that those who have met the second death are now burning in the great lake of fire or molten magma, where all dead souls go, and I was so stunned by what I saw.

All of us who are still alive are blessed with everlasting life and we will continue to have life as we get born again or reincarnate for as long as we follow all the Commandments of God. We are given free will and it is for us to decide whether we follow the path towards immortality or to break all the recommended guidelines for our lives and go towards the demise of our souls to burn in the lake of fire. The suicide bombers who killed innocent victims have chosen to end their lives forever, but their innocent victims are not dead but will be born again. Jesus told us to forgive; to be humble, to love your enemy, to turn your other cheek because it is only by doing so that we are prevented from killing which is the most grievous of all transgressions that will surely lead one to the lake of fire. On the other hand, the false prophet bade his followers not to show mercy to the enemy, to smite the neck of those who do not follow their beliefs, to take them for ransom, to divide their loot and these are the doctrines from a false god designed to lead one who follows them to the lake of fire.

The science community is trying so hard to disprove the existence of God even if at the very end of their quest for the truth, they always end up against a wall where they can no longer explain further why things are the way they are. I challenge them to disprove me. Despite these skepticisms of the science community, God showed me that science is indeed the truth and God bids us to believe nothing but the truth to attain intellectual perfection. God showed me that the seals that had been broken mentioned by John in the Revelation refer to all the achievements and scientific discoveries that had illuminated our understanding of our world, which contributed immensely towards the advancement of our knowledge. Those who had persevered to know the truth found the truth and God showed me that they were all given divine assistance to help us reach our destiny. The science community will not accept this but this is what Jesus meant when he said, "*Seek and you shall find.*"

Pura Regalado

Thrust in thy sickle and reap for the time is come for thee to reap for the harvest of the earth is ripe. Revelation 14:15

www.ingramcontent.com/pod-product-compliance
Lightning Source LLC
Chambersburg PA
CBHW051515120626
46551CB00012B/927